DAY OF THE MOON SHADOW

TALES WITH ANCIENT ANSWERS TO SCIENTIFIC QUESTIONS

Judy Gail
and
Linda A. Houlding

Illustrated by Kimberly Louise Shaw

LIBRARIES UNLIMITED, INC.
Englewood, Colorado
1995

LIBRARIES UNLIMITED, INC.
and its division Teacher Ideas Press
P.O. Box 6633
Englewood, CO 80155-6633
(800) 237-6124

Production Editor: Tama J. Serfoss
Copy Editor: Ramona Gault
Proofreader: Suzanne Hawkins Burke
Layout and Design: Michael Florman

Library of Congress Cataloging-in-Publication Data

Gail, Judy.
    Day of the moon shadow : tales with ancient answers to scientific
questions / Judy Gail, Linda A. Houlding ; illustrated by Kimberly
Louise Shaw.
    xx, 287 p. 22x28 cm.
    ISBN 1-56308-348-5
    1. Tales. 2. Manners and customs. 3. Nature study.
4. Multicultural education.   I. Houlding, Linda A.   II. Title.
GR76.G35 1995
306′.07--dc20   95-17642
                                                         CIP

To my late parents, Lillian and Hecky Krasnow
for their creative and loving upbringing, always and
forever an inspiration.
To my wonderful grandchildren, Timothy and Andrew Markewich
who love stories, songs, good books—and Grandma.
And to perseverance, my faithful companion.

—Judy Gail

To all children (young and old)
in whose imaginations these stories will live again and again.
To Captain Charles W. Houlding, USAF, whose unquenchable
interest in languages, oriental cultures, carnivorous plants, and
dinosaurs is a life-long catalyst and inspiration.
And especially to my sons, Ryan and Jason.

—Linda A. Houlding

CONTENTS

 LIST OF SONGS

 # ACKNOWLEDGMENTS

Grateful acknowledgments and many thanks go to the following:

- The Australian consulate general, New York, for films and pamphlets regarding Australian Aboriginal life;

- David Chikzaidze, cultural attaché at the former Soviet embassy in Washington, D.C., for the wealth of information he offered regarding the Georgian Mountaineers and the people of Khevsoureti, their customs, language, foods, clothing, ethnic backgrounds, homes, and history and for supplying authentic names for the characters in "The Khevsouri and the Cure," the folklore regarding the Eshmahkie, and the music of the region;

- The Florida Museum of Natural History in Gainesville for its information and exhibits on Native American life;

- The Morikami Museum in Delray Beach, Florida, for its wonderful exhibit on Japanese daily life and the detailed information given regarding the evil forest spirit, the Jikkinninnki (including the proper spelling);

- The Science Museum of Minnesota for its fact-filled "Volunteer Training Packet" and its scholarly and fascinating exhibit, "Wolves and Humans";

- Dr. Florentine Maurrasse, paleontologist and geologist at Florida International University, who spent several days showing us fossils and describing the science of paleontology and the history of the search for dinosaur bones;

- Anita Brown, band director at Clarkstown High School North, New York, for her original, meticulous, and impeccable hand-written transcriptions of the 73 songs in this book, which made transferring them onto computer possible within necessary deadlines;

- Temujin Ekunfeo, African storyteller and ethnologist for his fascinating account of and demonstration on the talking drum;

- Hawaiian storyteller, speaker, and poet, Makia™ Malo, for his description of Hawaiian sleds and the *holua* slide;

- Hutia Kanapu, native Hawaiian and story consultant for "Pele's Revenge";

- Jode Shaw, C.P.A., a specialist in the field of entertainment with a talent for bringing together clients whose talents benefit one another, for introducing us to her sister, Kimberly Louise Shaw, who thrilled us with her art work and has illustrated this book;

- John Schreiber, licensed massage therapist, who gave many hours of his time to describe what it is like to be blind and how his other senses compensate for this handicap;

- Carrie Sue Ayvar, our storyteller colleague, and Carrie's children, Khalil and Soralee Ayvar, and their friends, Melissa and Nicole Szwanke, for their performances and creative homemade instruments and didjeridoo improvisations in the audio rendition of "Monsters of the Sky Land";

- Josh, Noah, Sam, and Sarah (children of Judy Gail), for always laughing both with and at their mother despite the fact that she often forgot whether she was their mother or Shamus O'Toole, Helga the Howler, Chullachaqui, and so on, and so on;

- Dr. Mark Hagmann, wonderfully *mad* scientist and Judy Gail's devoted husband, for his support on all levels, information on the science topics covered, and his unfailing sense of order, which helped immeasurably in the organization of this book; and

- Tama Serfoss, our editor, for her interest, enthusiasm, input, guidance, and support.

INTRODUCTION

The germinating seed for *Day of the Moon Shadow: Tales with Ancient Answers to Scientific Questions* was planted in 1978 when I was asked by Judy Thomas, music teacher and New York State Orff-Schulwerk coordinator, to create a concert in conjunction with a festival at Nyack Elementary School in Rockland County, New York. The festival was based upon the theme: What peoples have wondered about since time began. The concert followed this theme and combined songs and stories from cultures around the world.

In 1983, I moved to Miami, Florida, and was hired by the Miami Museum of Science as director of live science to create entertaining, educational demonstrations. Here, I met Linda A. Houlding, anthropologist and then curator of natural history. Linda and I shared a fascination about how ancient peoples around the world viewed life and its natural phenomena. We also shared a concern that many American children, nurtured on a diet of often violent and biased television, one spoken language, and the mass media campaign for conformity in dress, fads, and behavior, viewed those who differed from themselves with fear and lack of respect. I told Linda about the concert and the festival in Nyack. The premise behind both was to demonstrate the beauty of cultural diversity and how, though peoples' customs and beliefs may vary widely, human beings from all cultures have the same needs and question the same things about life and the world around us. I sang the concert's theme song, "I Wonder and Ask," for Linda. This song incorporated questions about the universe presented to me by the students at Nyack Elementary. I used these questions as a basis for writing the concert.

This conversation, and the questions in the song, inspired Linda and me to create a series of thoroughly researched programs calculated to develop respect for humankind's diversity by tapping into the innate wonder everyone possesses, while presenting other cultures' customs, rituals, beliefs, and folklore in an engaging fashion. Researched and written on our own time, we offered to present these programs at the museum.

Each program in this series, "Wonder with Me," focused on a specific phenomenon expressed in a "wonder question," for example: "What makes thunder?" "What causes the northern lights?" or "Why does a firefly glow?" First, through a scientific experiment, we answered how that phenomenon is scientifically or technologically explained today. Then we'd ask our audiences to turn on their imaginations and travel back in time to a particular culture. We presented information on that culture's customs, rituals, and beliefs. Then, addressing the phenomenon or wonder question, we'd explain how this culture, without the benefit of our scientific knowledge, answered the same question through myth and folktale. We stressed the importance of the storyteller as the oral culture's walking encyclopedia of history, values, and answers to questions and as the prime source of entertainment for the people before the advent of the printed word, radio, and of course, television. Imagining a world without television was the first major step in transporting our audiences to another time and place, in opening their minds to the fact that everyone does not live, or necessarily wish to live, as we do.

These programs were performed for more than 90,000 children, parents, teachers, and others. They were received with overwhelming enthusiasm and came to the attention of Joy Reese Shaw, then director of programming at PBS station WLRN/Miami. WLRN taped the programs live and aired them as a series. Many teachers called the station and asked for videos to use in the classroom. Tapes were made and distributed in the county libraries of south Florida. We also held a contest in which students could submit a wonder question accompanied by a science experiment answering this question, an essay on a specific culture, or an original tale based on a wonder question.

I left the museum at this point to write and produce television programs for WLRN and other local stations and to pursue my career as a storyteller and balladeer. A short time later, Linda moved to California. I continued to perform the programs Linda and I had written and performed together. Although it was necessary to alter the format of the performances to suit one performer instead of two, the response to the material continued to be equally enthusiastic. Linda and I, still in constant communication, felt it was time to adapt the exciting information and captivating stories and songs into a book. We believed that our years of research, the fascinating information we had acquired, and the intriguing characters and events we'd created in these tales should now be made available to children and people of all ages across the nation.

Our approach to creating and developing the programs from which this book has grown was twofold. Six of the 14 tales are completely original: "They Called Him Brother" (Naskapi Indian); "Spirits of the Dancing Dead" (Inuit); "Pele's Revenge" (Hawaiian); "Day of the Moon Shadow" (Maya); "The Magic of Shamus O'Toole" (Irish); and "Helga the Howler" (Viking). The other eight are original but were inspired by actual native folktales or legends: "The Thunder Drum" (West African); "The Sun's Consent" (Siksika Indian); "In Search of the Ayaymama Bird" (Peruvian); "The Khevsouri and the Cure" (Russian); "Monsters of the Sky Land" (Aboriginal Australian); "Kiku's Reflection" (Japanese), "The Blind Man and the Deaf Man" (India); and "John Henry and the Steam Drill" (American). In each case, while selecting the cultures, we tried to be as diverse as possible regarding locales, climate, era, and worldview about existence, nature, and survival.

In researching the six completely original tales, we first read about the cultures, seeking literature that would indicate the particular people's explanation of a specific natural phenomenon. For example, how did the Inuit explain the aurora borealis, or the ancient Hawaiians the cause of volcanoes? How could we relate the love of the Irish for music and their tales of the little people to the scientific explanation of how sound travels? The drum was important to many African cultures; what might it represent in nature? Through our research on a culture, we came up with the phenomenon that would serve as the wonder question. First, we investigated the phenomenon scientifically. Then we delved into the folklore regarding this phenomenon as well as the general folklore and anthropology of the culture. After this immersion in the culture, the stories literally wrote themselves as though we had lived in these cultures and were merely recording what we had experienced. We nearly forgot our real selves as we stepped into the shoes of those about whom we were reading and writing. We hope this will be the experience of those who see, hear, or read these stories.

In researching the tales inspired by the native folktales and legends, we selected a culture and read its folktales. Upon finding a tale in which a scientific phenomenon played a part, such as birdsong in the tale "In Search of the Ayaymama Bird," the five senses in "The Blind Man and the Deaf Man," the laws of physics in "John Henry and the Steam Drill," and dinosaur bones in "Monsters of the Sky Land," we investigated the science of the phenomenon and the culture from which the tale came.

In addition to this research, we contacted foreign embassies and consulates for their suggestions about films, videos, books, and articles that would further our research and for any other information they might be able to offer. The Australian consulate general sent us pamphlets and three films on aboriginal life, and I drew upon my two years of living in Sydney, Australia, and conversations I'd had with aborigines, their answers to my many questions, and the sound of the *didjeridoo*. When I heard the latter's unearthly drone ring out through the air of Sydney Harbor, I felt a primal surge that all things are possible—one answer is as good as the next. This experience shaped the character of Wingarooloo and further fostered my innate fascination with diversity.

The Soviet embassy offered assistance with our Russian tale, "The Khevsouri and the Cure," through David Chikzaidze, the cultural attaché in 1986. Mr. Chikzaidze happened to be a genuine Khevsouri. Through telephone conversations, in articles sent to us, and on an audiocassette of Georgian Mountain music, Mr. Chikzaidze offered exciting information about life in Khevsoureti and the Georgian Mountains and their peoples of many cultures. I called upon my own Russian heritage, family tales told, and my grandmother's various cures—including garlic—for illnesses from sore throats to hiccups.

Linda and I travelled to the ancient city of Chichén Itzá in Mexico's Yucatán penninsula to experience the Maya/Toltec ruins firsthand, visit museums, and ask questions before writing *Day of the Moon Shadow*. When we worked on the tale from India, John Schreiber, a blind licensed massage therapist helped considerably as he told us how the other senses compensate when one or more of the five senses are damaged. We tapped into the resources and knowledgeable people at the Florida Museum of Natural History in Gainesville for information regarding Native American life and lore; the Morikami Museum in Delray Beach, Florida, for insights into Japanese life and the forest spirit, the Jikkinninnki; and the Science Museum of Minnesota's dynamic and inspiring exhibit, "Wolves and Humans," for information about wolves, the relationship between man and wolf in different societies and throughout history, and life amongst the Naskapi Indians.

Linda's years of study and research on North American Plains Indians while obtaining her master's of science degree in anthropology inspired the adaptation of the Siksika "Scarface" legend and the information about Indian sign language and tribal existence. Reading extensively about the Japanese culture, Linda learned of the ancient Japanese fascination with reflections in mirrors and the *hotaru,* or firefly warriors, leading to "Kiku's Reflection." Linda's knowledge of Pele and other Hawaiian gods and customs, the Inuit beliefs regarding the northern lights, and African tribal life and the importance of masks and drums gave us a head start in the direction our research took.

As a balladeer, songwriter, and musician, I was compelled to include original songs and music in each story. The former *Folkways Music Catalogue,* now under the auspices of the Smithsonian Institute, served as a guide to the music from many of the cultures in the stories. Other music was found in libraries and in my own collection of songbooks and ethnic recordings, obtained largely from the collection of my father, Hecky Krasnow, who for many years was director and producer of the Children's Education and Record Department at Columbia Records.

As our research continued, the topic of violence appeared unavoidable. In one form or another, violent figures and events are inherent in the mythology or folklore of many cultures. However, the violence we encountered in our reading was not the senseless and brutal human violence prevalent in today's movies, television, and society. Most often, it was not human against human violence, such as that condoned today in the American media because it brings in big money, although at the expense of our children's and society's values. Rather, the violence we encountered was in the form of mythological or legendary representations of the power of nature. Giants, evil spirits, devils, and angry gods all represented the intensity, strength, and unpredictability of nature and natural forces—storms, floods, droughts, death, wild animals, and volcanoes—those events in life that we know of and, at times, can even forecast, but simply cannot control.

The evil Amazon forest spirit Chullachaqui in the tale "In Search of the Ayaymama Bird," represented for that Peruvian culture all the terrifying things that occur from time to time in the jungle. Legend carries Chullachaqui's character further in that he is also able to cast spells upon people, but only on his turf, in the jungle. The ghostly, ruthless Jikkinninnki in "Kiku's Reflection" also reflects the culture's fears of the dark and pathless forest and the dangers that lurk therein. One of the characteristics of India's Rakshasas, demigod demons hostile to humans, is that they enter people by tainting their food, reflecting a common problem in that country and one its citizens are concerned about. When herbal cures failed to heal in Russia's Georgian Mountains prior to the advent of antibiotics, what caused this failure? Without scientific answers, the devilish Eshmahkie became the area's folklore figure who caused such misery. Life contains controllable events and uncontrollable ones. As the Khevsouri says to his great-great-grandson in the Russian tale, "In life there is good and evil, happiness and sorrow, sickness and health. If we open ourselves to the garden of earth, we can find joy—and an answer and a cure for all things."

The violent characters or events in these tales simply reflect the frightening side of the duality of life itself. Stories in all cultures did much more than simply provide entertainment; they served as lessons, examples of proper behavior, and warnings about dangers. The presence of malicious and frightening characters deterred listeners from dangerous places and taught them to avoid behavior that might invite evil consequences. Through these stories, social norms were reinforced.

The human sacrifices of the Maya, Viking, and Hawaiian cultures evoke fear and horror in today's society. Yet we cannot write these out of history simply because such torture and violation of human rights are abhorrent to us today. Consciousness changes as civilizations change. We still live in a world of turmoil and wars. However, as technology brings the entire planet closer and closer together, global consciousness is growing stronger. Attitudes regarding the treatment of others are changing and will continue to do so. Our motive in including these frightening events, violent as they may seem to us today, is part and parcel of our attempt to transport our readers into the mindset of these ancient cultures, to give them insight into how and why the people of these cultures lived as they did. The Maya, Vikings, and Hawaiians believed in their pagan gods. They believed that human sacrifices would please and appease the gods, thus, protecting their people from the ravages of nature, often, in their ancient beliefs, caused by angry gods. Many of those who were offered to the gods believed that their sacrifice guaranteed that their life after death would be infinitely better. To understand these cultures, we must temporarily suspend our own beliefs and imagine ourselves existing in nonscientific times, with the culture's frame of mind and frame of reference.

The positive side of life's duality is demonstrated in these tales by the human spirit's drive to overcome adversity. The actions of various characters throughout the stories counteract the evil spirits or negative occurrences. Love and caring win out over the Chullachaqui in "In Search of the Ayaymama Bird" and the Jikkinninnki in "Kiku's Reflection" as the parents of Raina and Kiku risk their lives to search for their beloved children. Keok dares to defy the Spirits of the Dancing Dead to save Tatque, his wife-to-be. The caring and loyalty of siblings portrayed in "Pele's Revenge" by Kimo and Iollana even teaches Pele a lesson in humility. The Khevsouri single-handedly takes on the Eshmahkie to save the life of his great-great-grandson.

In some of the other tales, cleverness, wit, and knowledge counteract evil. Maya priest Ahcucumatz and his sons use mathematical calculations to defeat the warring Toltecs. The Viking Helga the Howler uses reason and observation to deduce the cause of the trials and tribulations encountered on her journey and uses what she has learned about the giants' fears to defy them. The little turtle in "The Thunder Drum" uses her clever mind to outwit the selfish leopard, Osebo, and save the land from a drought. Leprechaun Shamus O'Toole could use negative magic to turn Her Ladyship into a water buffalo but chooses instead to use his understanding of human nature and his knowledge of how sound travels to silence her awful singing.

Reverence for life prevails in the Naskapi tale, "They Called Him Brother," though Animal Master teaches this lesson in a momentarily terrifying episode. All creatures must kill to eat. This is a fact of life. Respecting this fact and not killing for reasons other than survival is a clear message in this story. In "The Sun's Consent," even Father Sun has one enemy he cannot conquer, indicating the vulnerability of *all* things in creation. In this tale, Dancing Brook's unwillingness to break her promise with Father Sun is symbolic of the reverence all living creatures must have for nature and for the interdependency of all living things.

Cooperation is the theme of India's "The Blind Man and the Deaf Man" as these two individuals combine forces to compensate for each other's handicapped senses. Working together, they outsmart the evil Raskshasas, and then use the jewels they find to establish a shelter where all those in need of sensory assistance may come for help. This story represents genuine philanthropy and acceptance of all people, despite handicaps. The Naskapi hunters, who work side by side with the wolf, display the benefits of humans acting in harmony with animals and nature. The abuse of the Sky Land by the kadimakara in "Monsters of the Sky Land" shows what can happen when the natural harmony, beauty, and abundance of nature is tampered with and there is no cooperation or respect between creatures and habitats.

The indomitable human spirit rises to its highest in "John Henry and the Steam Drill" as John dares to attempt—and achieves—the seemingly impossible. In all these tales, one or more characters reaches out with bravery, cleverness, love, and belief to achieve, overcome, survive, or save. Their actions reflect the social values and worldviews of the cultures in which they take place. These values and beliefs are the guidelines and expectations for good and noble behavior beneficial to the individual and to the society as a whole. Violence, while present in some of these stories, is not lauded by the primary characters. The violence within these tales differs greatly from the senseless violence of present day video games and television shows. Rather, it teaches morals and values within the context of the cultures portrayed.

This book is a wonderful stepping stone for classroom activities and discussions about the world of nature and existence. We recommend picking a wonder question and researching it in one or both of the manners described in this introduction. Let the students create their own science experiments, histories, or tales of cultures. The students' tales can be dramatized in play form with students acting out the roles of each character. Let the class look at pictures of the terrain of the cultures selected, what the people wear, what their houses look like, and what means of transportation they use. Develop an art project centered on the students' cultural studies. Studying cultures that use masks can lead to fun and exciting projects in which students learn about the significance of masks and then make their own. Paper bags, papier-mâché, drawing paper, or cardboard are inexpensive and readily available materials for such a project.

A science experiment and brief talk about the culture should precede each tale. There are many excellent books that can serve as aids in creating these experiments. Books are available at the library, through book catalogs, bookstores, and stores such as The Nature Company or World of Science, both of which have excellent catalogs from which these can also be ordered. Some of these resources are listed in the reference sections at the end of each chapter. Likewise, many wonderful books of folklore and folktales are available in the library. Each chapter in this book covers science, cultural anthropology, and folktales and thus can inspire activities in science, history, and language arts.

Music can also be incorporated with the tales. Have the students listen to music from a culture and let them use basic percussion instruments as accompaniment. If a student or teacher can play the piano, there is a wide array of electronic keyboards available that offer a host of different rhythms and ethnic sounds. The guitar also is a versatile instrument and serves well for many of the tales. Let the students move to the percussive and musical sounds, and if a story incorporates a tribal or village celebration, let these movements develop into dances that the students themselves choreograph or improvise. The tales in this book inspire activities in the exciting art of storytelling. Our reference sections also suggests some books that detail fun projects to promote and encourage storytelling in the classroom, within the family, and amongst individuals.

An audiocassette of four selected tales and six songs from the text of the book may be purchased. It was most difficult to decide which tales and songs to record in the limited time that a 90-minute cassette offers, for all fourteen stories in the book reflect totally different cultures in theme, characters, story, and music. We finally decided to take listeners to four geographical corners of the earth: Australia in "Monsters of the Sky Land," Central America in "Day of the Moon Shadow," Asia in "Kiku's Reflection," and northern Europe with "Helga the Howler." Also included is a sample of songs from the tales of Ireland, Russia, the Siksika Indians, the Inuit, India, and West Africa. Those wishing to obtain audiocassettes of the 10 tales not included on the Libraries Unlimited cassette may purchase additional tapes directly from Poppykettle Enterprises, Inc., 13411 SW 112th Ln., Miami, FL 33186, (305) 387-3683.

Who is this book for? Our experience performing these chapters as live programs taught us that the subject matter is of interest to people of all ages and from all walks of life. Linda and I will never forget how we trembled in our shoes the day 200 Boy Scouts arrived at the museum one summer. Their abundance of energy manifested as they complained in unison and acted surly when they entered the auditorium to hear "dumb, baby stories." In less than five minutes, silence filled the air as these 200 Boy Scouts became utterly captivated. At the end, they walked out chanting the Siksika "Eh o eh o" chant. They later returned for the next show!

Each story offers new knowledge to most people. How many adults, for example, knew before reading this book that Hawaiians had sled races? How many knew how the Inuit view the northern lights, why animals killed with blowgun darts dipped in the poison curare can be eaten, that the Vikings believed in giants, that some people have lived well into their hundreds without vaccinations or antibiotics, or that a whole language was developed based on drums?

This book is for everyone fascinated by natural phenomena and people, for everyone who is filled with wonder and the questions it inspires. It is excellent enrichment for elementary school classrooms, for family reading and sharing, and for storytellers, both amateur and professional, who like to tell a good, suspenseful, informative tale. It is for those who enjoy musical tales filled with the drama of life. This book, with its accompanying audiocassette, is for all those who relish the beauty and wonder of the diversity of humankind and wish to gain deeper understanding, especially important now, as we move ever-forward toward a global world.

—Judy Gail

1
THE THUNDER DRUM

A Story from West Africa

How do the clouds and electricity
Make the lightning and thunder that we hear and see?
I wonder and ask, ask and wonder!

In 1752, Benjamin Franklin wanted to prove that lightning is electricity. He did this by conducting what was probably one of the most dangerous science experiments ever devised. Read about it here—but do not try it at home! Mr. Franklin flew a kite into the middle of a thunderstorm! He tied a metal key to the end of the wet string attached to the kite, put the key in a jar, and held onto the jar. His theory was indeed proven true when electricity from the storm cloud traveled down the string into the key. Luckily, Benjamin Franklin, great scientist, statesman, and author, survived to tell about his discovery! A few months later, a French scientist was killed trying to duplicate Franklin's experiment.

Lightning, one of the most powerful forces on earth, is nothing more than a huge electric spark. You can create your own miniature lightning by scuffing your shoes across a carpet and immediately touching something metal or another person. The spark that jumps from your finger to the metal or the unfortunate person, giving both of you a small shock, is static electricity.

Static electricity builds up inside a thundercloud. When this build-up occurs, a giant spark jumps from one part of the cloud to another, or from one cloud to another, or even from the cloud to the ground below. Thus, a magnificent bolt of sheer power—lightning—is born!

Magnets can help us to better understand lightning. Magnets have poles. Opposite poles, that is, positive and negative poles, attract each other and pull together. Like poles, positive and positive or negative and negative, repel each other and push the magnets apart. Electricity works the same way. Positive and negative charges of electricity attract each other. Negative and negative or positive and positive charges of electricity repel each other.

The water vapors that make up clouds contain electric charges, some negative and some positive. Opposite charges are drawn together, releasing thousands and thousands of electric sparks, millions, perhaps even billions, of times stronger than the sparks we get from scuffing our shoes across the carpet. That is why lightning is so dangerous.

Lightning causes a sometimes scary but harmless phenomenon: thunder. Thunder occurs when a bolt of lightning heats the air around its path by several thousands of degrees. The air molecules rapidly become excited and push out, violently bumping into each other. The resultant sound wave is the crash we hear as thunder!

Light travels at 186,000 miles per second—much faster than sound, with a speed of 0.2 (or ⅕) miles per second. Knowing this, we can calculate how far away a bolt of lightning has struck. Count the seconds between the lightning's flash and the thunder's crash. Divide this number by five. Your answer will be the number of miles away that the lightning struck.

All of this electrical activity and commotion among the clouds alters the state of the water vapors in the clouds, and these vapors then fall to earth as rain. If lightning and rain do not occur for a long time, the land suffers a condition known as drought. In a drought, plants wither and die because they receive no water to make them grow. Without plants, herbivorous, or plant-eating, animals have no food and die. The carnivorous, or meat-eating, animals then have no herbivorous animals to eat. Plants, animals, and people suffer from thirst and hunger. Thousands of years ago, before people knew about electrical charges, they wondered why there was lightning and thunder, and, if there was a drought, why?

Imagine yourself going back to that time to visit a village on the vast and varied Ivory Coast of Africa. There is green, lush jungle everywhere. In the center of this foliage is a clearing, and in this clearing is King Bashu's village, with 20 huts surrounding King Bashu's hut. A few miles away, yet still part of King Bashu's tribe, is another village with about 10 huts, and then some miles farther, another village with 5 huts. The huts are made from sticks and dried mud. They are comfortable and help keep people cool in the jungle heat. The tribes grow vegetables and hunt animals for meat. Their favorite vegetable is the sweet potato.

Enter King Bashu's hut. He has an urgent problem. The scouts who guard the village have informed him that the village is surrounded by enemy warriors who are about to attack. The king must send out a warning. There is no electricity, radios, televisions, or telephones. King Bashu could send smoke signals, but for the many miles that the message must travel, this would take too long. But he knows just what to do. He sends the message using drums! The drums "talk" as the varying beats and rhythms say different things.

The drums King Bashu and his tribe use do not look like the drums we commonly see played in jazz and rock bands. They vary in size and shape. Some are enormous—reaching 10 feet long and 10 feet wide! The sounds from these drums carry up to 20 miles. The members of the tribe, spread out in their clusters of huts, understand the different signals, almost like a Morse code. Though the rhythms do not spell out actual words, they convey messages, and not only messages of war.

For example, a mother in the village five miles away gives birth to a baby boy. The proud parents want everyone in the tribe to know this. They might beat *boom boom boom—ba ba boom—boom boom ba ba ba!* Were the baby a girl, the beats might be *ba ba boom—boom boom boom—ba ba ba boom boom!* Or the hunters return with an antelope, and King Bashu wants to invite everyone to a celebration feast. The drums might say *bam bada bam bam boom da da bam*, with some notes played with low timber and others with a higher pitch, for the tones of the drums can be altered greatly. When Africans were brought to America as slaves, they were forbidden to play drums, because their masters could not understand the drum language and feared drums could be used to spread word of uprisings and other trouble.

In the days of King Bashu, television and the printing press have not yet been invented. There are no books to read, no computer games, movies, or radios. His tribe has its own special form of entertainment. At night, when all the day's work is done, the entire tribe gathers around the central meeting area and acts out a play. Sometimes, this play is ceremonial, and only the men are in it. Many times, everyone participates—even the children. Music is very important, and each character has its own song to sing and mask to wear. The masks represent good spirits, bad spirits, animals, and gods.

Most important of all, the tribe has its storyteller, usually an old man or woman. The storyteller is a walking encyclopedia of tribal history and tales. The stories told serve many important purposes. They provide entertainment and offer lessons in tribal history. They indicate proper behavior—what is good or bad, acceptable or not acceptable. On the nights of storytelling, great excitement fills the air. Masks are prepared, and the musicians and dancers chant, sing, and play drums and other percussive instruments as the storyteller recites tales.

King Bashu's tribe believes in a sky god named Nyamey. Nyamey first lit a sky fire, which was lightning, and then beat on his large drum, which made thunder. Because of this, the land was blessed with rain. King Bashu acts the part of Nyamey at the storytelling fest. His mask has holes running along each side. Through these, King Bashu hangs straw streamers made from jungle plants and painted vivid colors. The mask is extremely heavy, but the king holds it on by biting a wooden piece in the underside of the mask with his strong jaw. He cannot speak with this in his mouth but grunts as the storyteller speaks the words.

Imagine yourself under a sky filled with a myriad of bright stars, more numerous than any seen in a modern city or suburb, for electricity interferes drastically with this clear vision of celestial grandeur. As always, the plays begin with the children asking questions of the storyteller. A big fire burns in the center of the circle. With everyone's belly full of antelope meat and sweet potatoes, and the men imbibing a special drink to fire up their souls and call upon the spirits, the storyteller begins.

THE THUNDER DRUM

Children, tonight you have asked, "What would happen if somebody stole the drum of Nyamey, the sky god?" This did happen many moons and stars ago. Nyamey's drum was stolen by a selfish, mean, ferocious leopard named Osebo. This Osebo had stolen Nyamey's drum, and Nyamey could not beat the drum to bring the thunder and the rain. The Land of the Drum People was suffering a terrible drought. Plants dried and died. Animals were thirsty, starving, and dying. The Drum People were sick, dying, and very sad.

Yet, each day the people and the animals went to the watering hole to meet and dig beneath the hot, dry sand for whatever moisture droplets remained. And every day, despite their thirst and hunger, they were polite to one another and greeted each other in their language of Swahili. *"Jambo!"* they'd say. *"Jambo!"* means "Hello, how are you, and good day; have an even better evening!" They sang

> *Jambo! It means "How are you?"*
> *Jambo! It means "Good day!"*
> *Jambo! It means "How are you?"*
> *Jambo! It means "Good day!"*

The day my tale begins, all the animals and Drum People were gathered at the watering hole when the heavens opened and Nyamey the sky god appeared. "Woe upon the land! We are drying and dying. What will we do?" He looked around the watering hole and spotted the elephant. "Elephant, you are the largest animal in the land. You have a very tough skin. I, your sky god, command you to go to the home of selfish Osebo the leopard and get my drum that I may roll the thunder and bring the rain!"

Now, the elephant knew that he had to obey Nyamey's command, and he set off through the jungle toward the ferocious leopard's home.

> *I am an elephant. I am BIG!*
> *I have a very tough skin!*
> *Nyamey the sky god bids me get the drum from Osebo, the leopard,*
> *And I am scared, oh, so scared.*

And well he should have been, for when the elephant reached Osebo's home, Osebo was sitting on the stolen drum like a mean king on a mean

---

throne. When he saw the elephant coming, he roared, "Why are you here? I don't like visitors!"

"Osebo, you cannot be so selfish! The land is drying and dying. You must give me Nyamey's drum so he may roll the thunder and bring the rain!"

And do you know what that leopard did? He roared and leaped off the stolen drum, chasing the elephant and even managing to dig his sharp claws into the thick skin of the elephant's hind leg! But fortunately for the elephant, Osebo remembered he had left the stolen drum unattended. Afraid somebody would steal it from him, he let the elephant go and ran back to the drum.

When the elephant returned to the watering hole, Nyamey looked down and said, "You do not have my drum! Woe upon the land. What will we do?" And he looked around the watering hole and spotted the antelope. "Antelope, you are the swiftest animal in the land. Why, you can run faster than anyone, even Osebo. You could snatch my drum from under him and run, run, run with it. I, your sky god, command that you go to the home of selfish Osebo and get my drum that I may roll the thunder and bring the rain!"

Now the antelope knew he had to obey the command of the sky god, and he set off through the jungle toward the ferocious leopard's home.

I am an antelope. I am swift!
I am the fastest one in the land!
No one runs faster than I can!
But I am scared. Oh, so scared.

And well he should have been, for, when Osebo saw the antelope coming, he roared, "Don't tell me you've come to get my drum. I'll never give it up! Never! Ever! Never!"

The antelope replied, "Osebo, you cannot be so selfish! You have three drops of water left in front of your home and one green leaf. But soon the drought will get to you, too, and you will have no drops of water and no green leaf. You must give me Nyamey's drum that he may roll the thunder and bring the rain!"

And do you know what the leopard did? He roared and leaped off the stolen drum, chasing after the antelope. Fortunately for the antelope, he was much faster than Osebo, and once again, Osebo remembered he had left the stolen drum unattended and was afraid somebody would steal it from him.

But when the antelope reached the watering hole, Nyamey looked down and said, "You do not have my drum. Woe upon the land, for now we are surely doomed!" And he rose back up into the heavens! But just before he disappeared entirely, he heard a little voice saying, "Nyamey, Nyamey, I will get the drum!"

Nyamey looked down, and do you know what he saw talking to him? An eensy, beensy, weensy, teensy, squishy, meek, and mild little turtle! For, as the story goes, in those days, turtles did not have shells. Nyamey said, "If the big, tough-skinned elephant could not get my drum, and the swift antelope could not get my drum, how are you, an eensy, beensy, weensy, teensy, squishy, meek, and mild little turtle going to get it?"

"I do not know, but I must try, or we will die!"

"Go then," Nyamey answered, "and forgive me for doubting you. Yes, go! You are our last hope! Go with my blessings!" And the little turtle set off through the jungle toward Osebo's home.

I am just a little turtle,
A very, very little turtle.
I must get Nyamey's drum,
For thunder and rain, you must come!

I am just a little turtle.
I do not know what I will do.
I know I must think of something,
For thunder and rain, we need you.

And just at that moment, the turtle got an idea and did something turtles had never done before and have never done since. She leaped and hopped and ran—she practically flew to the home of the ferocious, mean, selfish leopard! When Osebo saw the squishy little turtle, he was about to roar, but instead he laughed. "Rrr, rr, r, har, rah, harrrr, ruff, roaf, harrrrr, rrharr! I don't believe it! I just don't believe it. Don't tell me they sent you to get my drum!"

"Oh, why no, Osebo. I didn't come to get your drum. I came to prove that your drum is not the biggest drum in the land!"

When he heard this, Osebo, who always had to be the biggest and the best, always right and perfect, stood up on his hind legs, lifted his front paws, and was about to dig his sharp claws into the squishy, meek, and mild little turtle. But the turtle said, "No! No, no, no! Osebo, w-w-wait! If your drum is really the biggest drum in the land, you can prove it to me!"

And the leopard, who always had to prove he was right about everything, puffed up his chest, put down his front paws, and roared, "How?"

"Well, Osebo, you know the big hole in the bottom of your drum? If your drum is really the biggest drum in the land, you can fit inside the big hole in the bottom of it!"

And the leopard, who always had to prove he was right about everything, immediately put his head in the big hole in the bottom of the drum and roared, "That proves it! Now, get me out of here. It's hot!"

"Oh, no, Osebo, if your drum is really the biggest drum in all the land, then you can fit your front legs and your middle section inside the big hole in the bottom of your drum!"

And Osebo, who always had to prove he was right about everything, immediately put his front legs and his middle section into the big hole in the bottom of the drum and roared, "That proves it! Now get me out of here. It's hotter than hot sauce in here!"

"Oh, no, Osebo, if your drum is really the biggest drum in the land, you can fit your back legs and your backside into the big hole in the bottom of the drum!"

And Osebo, who always had to prove he was right about everything, immediately squiggled his back legs and his backside into the big hole in the bottom of the drum and roared, "That's it! That proves it! Now get me out! It's hot as an inferno in here!"

"Uh, oh, Osebo, your tail is sticking out!" And the leopard slammed his tail into the big hole in the bottom of the drum.

In the meantime, the clever little turtle took every last drop of saliva from her drying mouth, mixed it with the three drops of water left in front of Osebo's home, and, from the one green leaf, milked every last drop of moisture—and she made a mud pie! She slapped the mud pie onto the big hole in the bottom of the drum, and, in the hot, dry, drought sun, in one split second, it turned into the hardest clay pack ever, and Osebo was trapped inside the stolen drum. And did he ever ROOOAAARRR, "Get me out of here!"

But the little turtle, knowing that she had saved the land, was so filled with joyous energy, she rolled the drum with Osebo in it all the way back to the watering hole singing

From *Day of the Moon Shadow: Tales with Ancient Answers to Scientific Questions.*
©1995. Libraries Unlimited. (800) 237-6124.

I am just a little turtle,
A very, very little turtle.
But I got the drum from Osebo,
And, HA! I got Osebo, too!

When the turtle returned to the watering hole, everybody rejoiced, and Nyamey immediately lit the sky fire, which was lightning. But no one could hear themselves or anyone else over the roaring of the leopard. "Let me out of here now! Get me ooouuut!"

Nyamey replied, "I will use my magic powers to open the drum—on one condition, Osebo. You must promise never to inflict such misery upon the plants, animals, people, and our good land again! You must never steal my drum, or, for that matter, the drum of any person in the Land of the Drum People!"

"All right! All right! All right! I promise. Just get me out of here!"

And Nyamey used his magic and opened the drum. Osebo crawled out and hung his head in terrible shame, apologizing to plants, animals, people, and the land for what he had done. Nyamey lifted the drum up into the heavens, letting the thunder roll loud and strong. But before he let the rain fall, he spoke: "Turtle, for your bravery and cleverness, I grant you a reward. What is it you would wish?"

And what do you think the turtle asked for? She said, "I would wish for a shell, a hard shell that I could carry with me as my house to find shelter and safety inside!" And down from the heavens, Nyamey brought a beautiful painted shell and placed it upon the turtle's back, and, as the story goes, from this day onward, turtles have had their shells!

With the shell upon the happy turtle's back, Nyamey let the raindrops fall. All the Drum People and animals opened their mouths and drank the water. Plants and flowers rose and opened their leaves and petals toward the sky. The dry earth turned rich red and brown once again as the land drank the water. And the Drum People played their drums and danced and sang along with the animals

Rain, rain, rain, rain,
Rain, rain, rain, rain!
Jambo, Jambo, Jambo, Jambo!
Jambo, Jambo, Jambo, Jambo!

From *Day of the Moon Shadow: Tales with Ancient Answers to Scientific Questions.*
©1995. Libraries Unlimited. (800) 237-6124.

References

Science

- Arvatia, Chris. 1985. *Why Does It Thunder and Lightning?* Chicago: Childrens Press.

- Harre, Rom. 1981. *Great Scientific Experiments*. Chap. 18. Oxford: Phaidon Press.

- *The New Book of Knowledge*. 1987. Danbury, CT: Grolier.

- *Thunderstorm Morphology and Dynamics*. 1986. 2d ed., rev. and enl. Norman: University of Oklahoma Press.

- Uman, Martin A. 1986. *All About Lightning*. New York: Dover.

Anthropology

- Blinkenberg, Christian Sorensen. 1911. *The Thunderweapon in Religion and Folklore, a Study in Comparative Archaeology*. Cambridge: The University Press.

- Davidson, Basil. 1967. *African Kingdom*. New York: Time Life.

- Diallo, Yaya, and Mitchell Hall. 1989. *The Healing Drum—African Wisdom Teachings*. Rochester, VT: Destiny Books.

- Feelings, Muriel L. 1974. *Jambo Means Hello; Swahili Alphabet Book*. New York: Dial Press.

- Moore, Clark D., and Ann Dunbar. 1968. *Africa, Yesterday and Today*. Bucks County, PA: Bantam Books.

- Rittner, Marciline K., and William Arnett. 1978. *Three Rivers of Nigeria*. Atlanta, GA: High Museum of Art.

Folklore

- Courlander, Harold. 1957. *The Hat Shaking Dance and Other Tales from the Gold Coast*. San Diego: Harcourt Brace Jovanovich. ("The Thunder Drum" was inspired by the traditional tale "Osebo's Drum" found in this source.)

- ———. 1975. *A Treasury of African Folklore*. New York: Crown.

- Gale, Stephen H. 1995. *West African Folktales*. Lincolnwood, IL: NTC Publishing Group.

- Holiday, Virginia. 1970. *Bantu Tales*. New York: Viking.

- Rugoff, Milton, ed. 1949. *A Harvest of World Folktales*. New York: Viking.

Music

- Ella Jennkins, Jambo. *More Call and Response Chants*. Folkways FC 7653.

- *Ewe Music of Ghana*. Folkways 4222.

- Seeger, Pete, and The Weavers. *Bantu*. Folkways FP 912.

Jambo!

From "The Thunder Drum"

Music and Lyrics by
JUDY GAIL

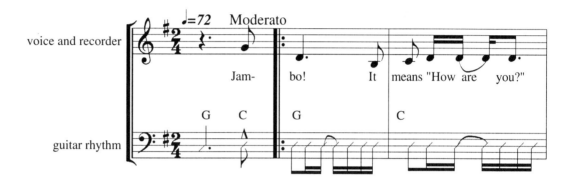

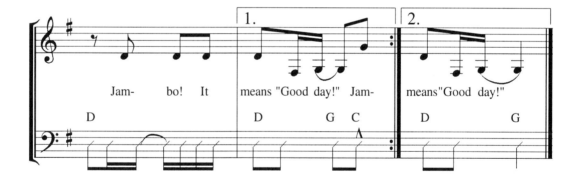

The Elephant's Song

From "The Thunder Drum"

Music and Lyrics by
JUDY GAIL

The Antelope's Song

From "The Thunder Drum"

Music and Lyrics by
JUDY GAIL

The Turtle's Song

From "The Thunder Drum"

Music and Lyrics by
JUDY GAIL

The third verse should be sung fast and joyously after the turtle gets the drum.

2. I am just a little turtle.
   I do not know what I will do.
   I know I must think of something,
   For thunder and rain, we need you.

3. I am just a little turtle,
   A very, very little turtle.
   But I got the drum from Osebo,
   And, HA! I got Osebo, too!

Finale: Rain Song and Jambo

From "The Thunder Drum"

Music and Lyrics by
JUDY GAIL

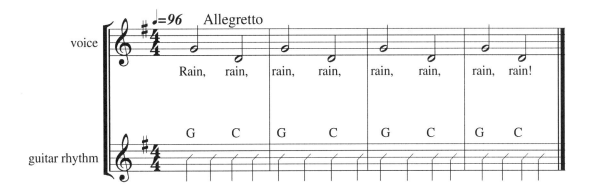

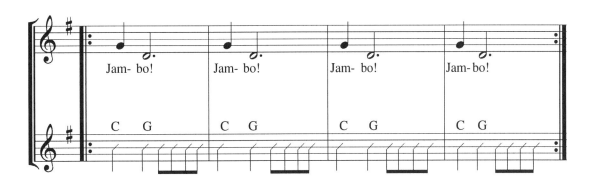

2
THE SUN'S CONSENT

A Story from the Siksika, or Blackfoot Indians, of North America

How does the sun create things organic?
So life teems and blossoms upon earth, our planet?
I wonder and ask, ask and wonder!

The sun is 93 million miles from the earth! Despite the overwhelmingly vast distance, this gaseous ball of fiery nuclear activity is the source of life for our planet. Photons, which are bundles of energy found in light, stream from the sun and shine on green plant life. The green color in plants is caused by a chemical called chlorophyll. Chlorophyll catches the light energy and turns it into chemical energy, helping plants to make sugars out of air and water. This process is called photosynthesis. The plants then use the sugar they make to grow and reproduce and store extra sugars and starches. People and animals eat these plants and use the sugars and starches as food for their own energy and growth.

Plants are the basis for intricate food chains that ultimately feed almost every living thing on our planet. A food chain is a map that shows what eats what in any given habitat. It is also a flow chart showing where the sun's original energy goes. At the bottom of the food chain are the primary producers. These are the plants that make their own food. Next are the primary consumers, the animals who eat the plants. They are called herbivores. Next come the secondary consumers, animals who eat the primary consumers. They are called carnivores. When animals excrete the remains of their meals, the feces contain air and water. This excretion completes the food chain by returning to the earth the air and water that the plants originally used to make their sugars.

Let's put the food chain in other words. Think of a cow and a bull walking in a field of clover. They eat the clover, and their bodies convert this food into energy, allowing them to breathe, walk, moo, snort, and stay alive. People come along, milk the cow, and from the milk make cheese, butter, and cream. They drink the milk and put butter and cheese on a piece of bread. The bread is made from wheat, which, like the clover, grows because of photosynthesis, which occurs because of sunlight. Then, people eat hamburgers made of meat obtained from the bull that has eaten the clover, which has survived because of those photons of light from the sun reacting with the chlorophyll in the clover's cells. The people convert the food they have eaten into energy in order to walk, talk, invent, play computer games, draw, dance, calculate mathematics, fly airplanes, and so on. All this energy originated from the sun.

If a planet is too close to the sun, the light and heat may be too great to allow life to exist. If a planet is too far from the sun, the light and heat will not be strong enough to allow life to exist. The amounts of oxygen, carbon dioxide, and water on the planet also affect whether life can exist. The earth is blessed with all of these necessities and is the right distance from the sun to work in harmony with it.

Today, thanks to high-powered telescopes and the knowledge that astronomers have gained about the sun, we know that the sun is a star and that stars have life cycles—baby, middle age, and old age. We know that our sun is middle-aged and still has billions of years of life left. We know that the planets revolve around the sun in specific orbits. We know about sunspots and flares. Hundreds of years ago, people did not have this information. Every day, they would see the sun appear as a big ball of fire in the sky. Every night, they would see it travel away, looking as though it sank into the ocean or fell over a mountain top. What was this big ball of fire to them?

Native Americans had some very powerful beliefs regarding the sun. They knew that life depended on this fiery sphere. The Blackfoot Indians, or Siksika, as they called themselves, of southern Alberta, Canada, worshipped the sun as Father of All Living Things. Every morning this great father would rise in the east, shedding warmth and light on Mother Earth as he journeyed across the heavens. The Blackfoot told many tales about brave warriors who visited Father Sun in his dwelling in the sky. Imagine yourself going back to the year 1820 to visit the Siksika in southern Alberta.

The Siksika spoke the Algonquian language. How can we communicate with them? They might think we are enemies. We must find a way to speak, and the best way is through sign language.

On the Great Plains in the middle of the United States, as well as in southern Alberta, there were huge herds of millions of big, hoofed animals—the bison, commonly called buffalo. Different Native American tribes rode their horses over the plains to hunt buffalo. Often, hunters from one tribe would run into hunters from another tribe. Usually, the tribes spoke different languages. That is one of the reasons Indians developed sign language. With these signs, all the tribes could communicate with one another.

Each tribe dressed and wore its hair differently. Some hair was braided, some was long and straight, and some was cropped short or shaved. From this, and from clothing design and decoration, a person from one tribe could tell which tribe another person was from and whether or not that person was a friend or an enemy. For an example of how the sign languages might work between tribes, imagine that a Pawnee comes upon a Cheyenne and notices that the Cheyenne has several fine moose skins. The Cheyenne and the Pawnee were traditional enemies, but if their tribes were not currently at war, they might decide to trade. The Pawnee signs that he wishes to trade his surplus corn for three of the skins (the Pawnee were one of the Great Plains tribes that practiced agriculture). The Cheyenne signs back that, if the Pawnee will also include his shirt decorated with colorfully dyed porcupine quills, he will agree to the trade. The Pawnee more closely examines the quality of the moose skins. Satisfied, he signs, "Yes, it is agreed."

Tribes like the Siksika were well-trained hunters. They listened for sounds in the distance and felt vibrations in the ground to learn when the buffalo were stampeding. The sound and vibrations in the earth told the hunters how near the herds were. Buffalo hunts were extremely dangerous! Highly skilled hunters used horses that they had trained to run alongside the huge, powerful buffalo. From their mounts, the hunters shot buffalo with bows and arrows.

The Siksika used the buffalo for almost all their needs. They ate the meat and used the skins to make tepee covers and clothing. They made tools out of the bones and necklaces and other jewelry from the teeth. Every part of the animal was used for something. Even buffalo droppings were gathered, dried, and burned for fuel. From the bladder, each family made a parfleche, a bag for carrying water and other items. They mixed dried buffalo meat, fat, and berries to make pemmican, a concentrated food that they carried on long journeys. Mixed with water, pemmican would make a hearty stew.

In the Siksika camps, all the tepees were arranged in a circle called the Sacred Life Circle. This circle symbolized that life has no beginning and no end, which is what these people believed. The entrance to each tepee faced east in order to greet Father Sun as he rose each morning. The Siksika believed in enjoying life. Though they often had to struggle to survive, they engaged in festivities and much laughter and joking. Each tribe had its storyteller, who told tales about the life and beliefs of the Siksika and their history. Gathered around large fires, as the odor of roasting buffalo meat rose into the air, the teller entertained and captured the imaginations of all who listened.

The Sun's Consent

Siksika people, happy people,
Wander through this life on land.
Maidens, braves, hunters, warriors,
Blackfoot courage they command!

One snowy winter evening, all the warriors of the tribe were sitting in Chief Lone Wolf's warm tepee around his cooking fire. They had just returned from hunting buffalo. One by one, each hunter told Chief Lone Wolf what he personally had done during the hunt. Now it was Scarface's turn to report. Scarface was a shy young man who had been born with a large ugly mark on his cheek. He spoke, "Shortly after the buffalo were sighted, my horse tripped over a loose rock and hurt her leg, and I was left without a horse to ride. On foot, I followed the warriors to the buffalo kill. Without a horse, I couldn't chase the buffalo, so I remained on the rim of the herd and shot them as they tried to escape. My arrows contributed four buffalo to the community!"

When Scarface finished, snickering was heard from three or four of the younger warriors. One called Nighthawk jumped up and said, "Ha! Not only is Scarface marred on his face, his brain also has a flaw. We all know he turned coward at the sight of so many great buffalo and ran like a rabbit back to the village. He only uses the story of his lame horse as an excuse!"

Everyone laughed as Scarface once again was made to appear the fool. It did not matter that Scarface's arrows had indeed been pulled from the hearts of four fine buffalo. Scarface suffered the brunt of their mocking jokes more often than was his share. He learned to accept this and usually joined in the laughter. This day, however, the sound of the laughter cut into his heart, for Dancing Brook, the chief's daughter, was in the tepee passing out buffalo stew to the men. At first, Scarface had been proud she could hear the story of his kill, but when the customary teasing began, he felt great alarm. He thought, "What if Dancing Brook believes Nighthawk's lies?" He hung his head in humiliation. Then he saw someone kneel next to him and lift his empty bowl. He looked up, straight into the eyes of Dancing Brook. She dipped into her pot for the largest piece of meat and put it into his bowl. Softly she spoke, "For the village's best meat provider and most honest warrior. Meet me by the river later tonight."

From *Day of the Moon Shadow: Tales with Ancient Answers to Scientific Questions.*
©1995. Libraries Unlimited. (800) 237-6124.

Scarface's glad spirit swelled in his chest until he felt he would burst. Dancing Brook believed in him! What did he care what the others said? Later that evening, as Scarface walked to the river, he sang his song of love.

My heart is like a bird.
It flies on open wings,
And soars just like the eagle
As Dancing Brook love brings.

The mean words of the braves,
This mark upon my face,
Did not blind my true love's eyes
Or in them me disgrace!

My heart is like the bird.
It flies on open wings,
And soars just like the eagle
As Dancing Brook love brings.

Soon Dancing Brook joined Scarface. From behind a bush they heard the voice of Nighthawk. "Ha!" he mocked. "If Dancing Brook will not marry someone handsome like me, then let her marry someone ugly like Scarface!"

Dancing Brook turned to Scarface and said, "I would love nothing more than to be your wife. But I have made a vow to Father Sun, giver of life to all creatures on Earth, our Mother. Only he can know which warrior has a true heart and seeks me out of love and not simply because I am the chief's daughter. So if you wish me as your wife, you must gain the Sun's consent."

"Then, my beloved Dancing Brook, I will get the Sun's consent! How do I get to the Land in the Sky? I do not know, but I will find the way or die trying!" Scarface returned to his tepee.

For several days Scarface's mother prepared him for his journey to the Sun's dwelling place in the sky. She made him a new and strong parfleche and filled it with much pemmican of buffalo meat, fat, and berries. She sewed him a pair of moccasins with intricate designs guaranteed to give him special powers on his journey. The day arrived for Scarface to set off toward the dwelling of Father Sun. All the villagers gathered to watch him as he left. They chanted the Siksika's Song of Courage.

From *Day of the Moon Shadow: Tales with Ancient Answers to Scientific Questions.*
©1995. Libraries Unlimited. (800) 237-6124.

Eh o eh o eh o eh o eh o eh o eh o eh!
Eh o eh o eh o eh o eh o eh o eh o eh!
Buffalo meat with fat and berries
Feeds my hunger night and day.
Moccasins will give me powers
On my journey, a long way.

Eh o eh o eh o eh o eh o eh o eh o eh!
Eh o eh o eh o eh o eh o eh o eh o eh!
Sun and moon and earth and sky
Guide me with their inner eye.
Mother Earth, oh, Earth our Mother
Gives me courage till I die!

Siksika people, happy people,
Wander through this life on land.
I am Scarface! I am warrior!
Blackfoot courage I command!
Eh o eh o eh o eh o eh o eh o eh o eh!
Eh o eh o eh o eh o eh o eh o eh o eh!

Scarface had been told that Sister Bear had great wisdom and might be able to help him find his way. He approached the lair of the She-Bear. "Chaah wheeewww. Chaah wheeewww!" Through the cold winter air, he could hear the snoring of the hibernating She-Bear. She slept so very deeply that Scarface could not wake her with his shouts and yelps. Finally, he slid right down into the She-Bear's lair and fell smack upon her head!

"Grrrr! How dare you wake me up from my hibernation! Prepare to be eaten!"

"No! No, Sister Bear! It is Scarface, brother to all creatures tame and wild. I have come for your wisdom!"

"My—wisdom? Ho ho! You think I'm that smart? Well, on second thought, don't prepare to be eaten! How can my—uhm—wisdom help you?"

"Sister Bear, I must get to the Sun's dwelling place in the Land in the Sky in order to get Father Sun's consent to marry Dancing Brook. I have no idea which way to go. Can you help me?"

"I think I just might be able to do so. That's a tough one, though. Let me think—you turn north—then—east, past the blue rock outcropping. Keep on walking until you come—hmmm—until you come to the Great Waters! That's as far as my wisdom can take you. From there it is between you and Father Sun. If he finds your heart worthy, he will find a way to get you to his dwelling place. Good luck, Brother Scarface—and please, do not wake me from my hibernation again. Chaah wheeewww—wisdommm."

Scarface followed the She-Bear's advice. For five days and nights he walked in the cold snow through chilling winds. As he walked, his heart spoke to Father Sun. "Please, oh great Father, please do not let me stop now. If I do not have Dancing Brook as my wife, my heart will break. A broken heart is like no heart at all. What good is a warrior without a heart?"

A warrior without a heart
Is like a deer without its ears
Is like a buff'lo without its hide
Is like a beaver without its teeth
Is like a rabbit that cannot hop!
Oh, Great Father, oh, Great Sun
Don't let me stop, don't let me stop!
Oh, Great Father, oh, Great Sun,
Don't let me stop, don't let me stop!

Finally, he reached the Great Waters, all sparkling and blue. He lay down to rest. After a while he awoke, for a chorus of birds was singing to him.

Arise, Scarface, wake up!
Sun Father's heard your prayer
As sure as you are hearing
Our voices through the air.

Arise, Scarface, wake up!
Sun Father waits for you
Across the Great Waters,
So wide, so deep, and blue.

Arise, Scarface, wake up!
Sun Father's heard your plea,
And offered his great powers
For you to cross the sea!

In front of the eyes of Scarface, the Milky Way, called the Wolf Trail, came down from the heavens to Earthland's side. Star by star, one star after another, Scarface climbed up until he reached the Land in the Sky, all beautiful, glowing, and golden. As he stepped into the radiance, he saw a handsome young brave dressed in white buckskin. His eyes twinkled like the stars in the heavens. The brave ran toward him, waving, "Hello, Scarface! My name is Morningstar. I am the child of the Sun. My father wishes me to take you to our dwelling place in the sky."

Morningstar led Scarface there. Mother Moon greeted him and said, "Welcome, Scarface. Father Sun will return soon from his journey around the earth, giving it the warmth of life and the light of day."

It was not long before Scarface felt surrounded by intense heat and magnificent energy. There, right before him, Father Sun appeared! He spoke, "Welcome to my Land in the Sky. I have allowed you to come here, for you will make a fine companion for my child, Morningstar. You may go exploring with him. You will find great beauty in my Land in the Sky. Unfortunately, there is one thing of which I must warn you—one evil that threatens my land—the knife-beaked bird monsters! They wish to kill my child, precious Morningstar. You may go where you wish, but stay away from these wretched monsters!"

The next day, Scarface and Morningstar set out. First they stayed side by side. Then they took separate paths. Scarface wished to join his friend again and followed the footprints he had made along the trail to find him. But his peaceful walk turned into one of terror when a dreadful screech filled the air! Looking up, Scarface cringed as a huge, vicious-looking bird with a long, sharp beak and talons far sharper than Sister Bear's claws swooped overhead. His eyes caught the motion of another bird as it swooped on something on the ground. He heard the cry of Morningstar and ran toward the pleading sound. There, on the ground, lay Father Sun's child, unable to move as one bird after another darted at him, tearing at his hair, pecking at his skin, shredding his clothing with their sharp beaks and talons!

Swiftly, Scarface took an arrow from the pack on his back. Carefully and steadily he aimed it at one of the birds, and his arrow found its mark. He took more arrows, pulled his bow taut, and shot down another and still another,

From *Day of the Moon Shadow: Tales with Ancient Answers to Scientific Questions.*
©1995. Libraries Unlimited. (800) 237-6124.

until only the evil leader remained. Scarface reached for another arrow, only to realize that he had none left. "What am I to do?" he thought.

Terrified, he ran to where his friend lay bleeding on the ground. Now the evil leader of the bird monsters swooped down on both of them. Scarface quickly pulled an arrow from the pack on Morningstar's back. His hands shook with terror. "I must," he chanted. "I can! I will!" He aimed the arrow at the monstrous bird. The arrow flew through the air and pierced the large creature, which fell with a shriek to the ground.

Scarface lifted Morningstar and carried him back to the dwelling place of Father Sun. Mother Moon nursed his wounds. Father Sun returned from his journey around earth, giving it the warmth of life and the light of day. He spoke: "I saw everything that happened today. Scarface, you are of one heart and one mind. You have saved the life of my child! For that I shall reward you. First, here is the Sacred White Buffalo Robe to be worn by those, and only those, blessed by the Sun. Its powers will protect you and bring you respect and honor for life! Second, you are now to be as my own child and the true brother of Morningstar! Third, my fine son, it is what shines forth from within you, not what is seen on the outside, that speaks of who you are. You are honest, loyal, and kind. From this moment on you shall no longer be known as Scarface but as Trueface! And now, my child, Trueface, tell me what brought you on this courageous journey to my dwelling place in the sky!"

Trueface knelt before Father Sun. "Oh, my Father, I thank you for your generosity and kindness. I am in love with Chief Lone Wolf's daughter, Dancing Brook. I wish to make her my wife, but she has vowed never to wed any man without your consent!"

"I can think of no better husband for Dancing Brook than you, my child. You have the Sun's consent to make her your wife!"

That Dancing Brook has kept her promise
Tells me that her heart is honest,
Tells me she knows I, the Sun,
Give warmth and life to ev'ryone!

From *Day of the Moon Shadow: Tales with Ancient Answers to Scientific Questions.*
©1995. Libraries Unlimited. (800) 237-6124.

You saved my child, blessed Morning Star.
You lived with pride despite your scar.
You did what others fear to do.
Come, Trueface, I will now bless you!

Rise and let my flames dance wild!
With joy I make you, too, my child!
My pow'rs and blessings make you strong
With Dancing Brook a whole life long!

Go now, go back to Siksika,
Dancing Brook, strong, happy people.
Go, my son, for I will guide
Brave warrior back to Earthland's side!

The Sun and Moon bid Trueface farewell. Morningstar led him back to the edge of the Land in the Sky. Again, the Milky Way, called the Wolf Trail, appeared. Star by star, Trueface descended to Earthland's side. He returned to the Siksika village. Following Siksika ritual, he remained on the hill, waiting for the villagers to come up and lead him down and into the village as though he were a total stranger.

The villagers gazed in awe, wondering who was the stranger wearing the Sacred White Buffalo Robe, for Trueface had wrapped himself full around in the robe, head and all. When he reached the bottom of the hill, he opened it. The villagers gasped! "Scarface! Surely, you have been blessed by Father Sun!"

"Indeed, I have. From this day forth, you are to call me Trueface, the name Father Sun, who calls me brother to his child, Morningstar, has given to me." Turning to Dancing Brook, Trueface announced, "Father Sun has granted me the greatest blessing of all! Dancing Brook, I have the Sun's consent to make you my bride!" Dancing Brook ran to her beloved, and they embraced.

For three days and nights, the people scurried about, preparing for the wedding feast. As they did so, their chants rang through the air. May the Great Spirit make the Sun rise in your hearts as you sing, too!

Eh o eh o eh o eh o eh o eh o eh o eh!
Eh o eh o eh o eh o eh o eh o eh o eh!
Eh o eh o eh o eh o eh o eh o eh o eh!
Eh o eh o eh o eh o eh o eh o EH O EH!

References

Science

- Asimov, Isaac. 1987. *How Did We Find Out About Sunshine?* (Force & Energy Series). New York: Walker.

- ———. 1972. *The Sun.* Follet Beginning Science Books.

- ———. 1971. *What Makes the Sun Shine?* (Atlantic Monthly Press Books). Boston: Little, Brown.

- Ellison, Mervyn Archdall. 1968. *The Sun and Its Influence: An Intro to the Study of Solar-Terrestrial Relations.* New York: American Elsevier.

- *Fire of Life.* 1981. (Smithsonian Exposition Books). New York: W. W. Norton.

- Halstead, Beverly. 1979. *A Closer Look at the Dawn of Life.* New York: Gloucester Press.

- Houston, David R. 1979. "Understanding the Game of the Environment." *Agricultural Information Bulletin* no. 426 (September).

Anthropology

- *America's Fascinating Indian Heritage.* 1978. New York: Reader's Digest.

- Hill, Tom, and Richard W. Hill, eds. 1994. *Creation's Journey: Native American Identity and Belief.* Washington, DC, and London: Smithsonian Institution Press.

- Kopper, Philip. 1986. *The Smithsonian Book of North American Indians: Before the Coming of the Europeans.* Washington, DC: Smithsonian Books.

- Spence, Lewis. 1914. *North American Indians.* London: Bracken Books.

- Tomkins, William. 1969. *Indian Sign Language.* New York: Dover.

Folklore

- Erdoes, Richard. 1976. *The Sound of Flutes and Other Indian Legends.* New York: Pantheon Books.

- Erdoes, Richard, and Alfonso Ortiz. 1984. *American Indian Myths and Legends.* New York: Pantheon Books.

- Hardin, Terri, ed. 1993. *Legends & Lore of the American Indians.* New York: Barnes & Noble Books.

- Norman, Howard, ed. 1990. *Northern Tales: Traditional Stories of Eskimo and Indian Peoples.* New York: Pantheon Books.

- San Souci, Robert. 1978. *The Legend of Scarface.* New York: Doubleday.

- Starr, Frederick. 1898. *American Indians: "Scarface," a Blackfoot Story.* Washington, DC: Heath.

Music

- *Music and Legend of the Blackfoot.* Folkways 4464 & 4541.

- *Music of the Algonkians.* Folkways 7753.

Song of Love

From "The Sun's Consent"

Music and Lyrics by
JUDY GAIL

This song may be accompanied by flute, guitar, or keyboard.

Siksika Song of Courage

From "The Sun's Consent"

Music and Lyrics by
JUDY GAIL

(The first two lines are sung at the beginning of the story.)

REPEAT CHORUS

REPEAT CHORUS

This song should be accompanied by a deep-sounding drum and a guitar strummed energetically in rhythm with the drum.

A Warrior Without a Heart

From "The Sun's Consent"

Music and Lyrics by
JUDY GAIL

Begin slowly . Repeat song 3x. Increase tempo with each repeat.

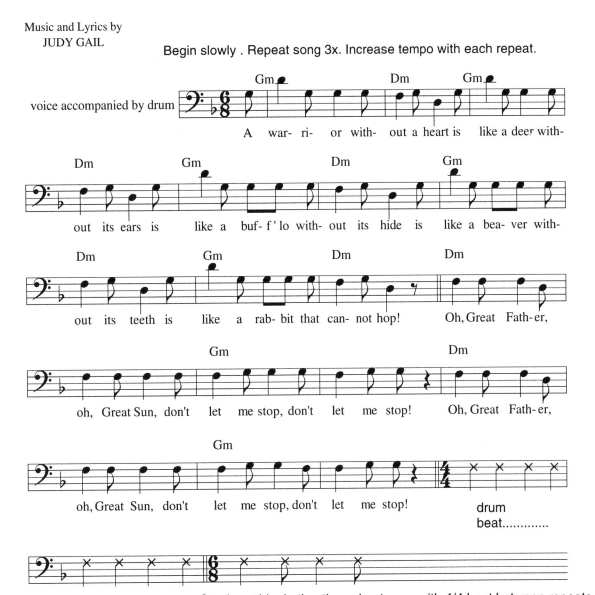

Continue this rhythm throughout song with 4/4 beat between repeats.

Song of the Birds

From "The Sun's Consent"

Music and Lyrics by
JUDY GAIL

Andante dolcissimo

1. A-rise, Scar-face, wake up! Sun Fath-er's heard your prayer as
2. A-rise, Scar-face, wake up! Sun Fath-er waits for you a-

sure as you are hear-ing our voi-ces through the air.
cross __ the Great Wa-ters, so wide, so deep, and blue.

3. A-rise, Scar-face, wake up! Sun Fath-er's heard __ your plea, and

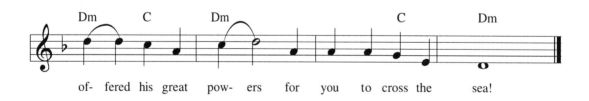

of-fered his great pow-ers for you to cross the sea!

This song may also be accompanied with guitar or keyboard.

The Sun's Consent

From "The Sun's Consent"

Music and Lyrics by
JUDY GAIL

Allegro con brio

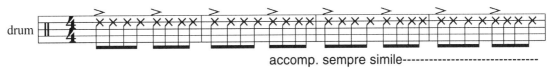

accomp. sempre simile-----------------------------

1. That   Dan-cing Brook has kept   her pro- mise tells me that her heart is hon- est,
2.   Rise and let   my flames dance wild! With   joy I make you, too, my child! My

tells   me she knows I,   the   Sun,   give   warmth and life to   ev'- ry- one!
pow'rs and bless-ings make you strong with   Dan- cing Brook a   whole life long!

1. You saved my child, blessed Morn-ing Star. You lived with pride de- spite your scar. You
2.   Go now, go back   to Sik- si- ka, Dan-cing Brook, strong, hap- py peo-ple.

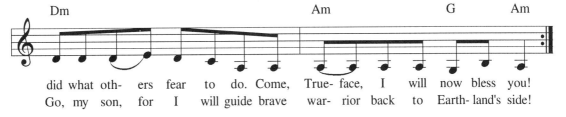

did what oth- ers fear to do. Come, True- face, I   will   now bless you!
Go, my son, for   I   will guide brave war- rior back to Earth- land's side!

This song should be accompanied by a drum on both verses.

3
IN SEARCH OF THE AYAYMAMA BIRD

IN SEARCH OF THE AYAYMAMA BIRD

A Story from Amazonian Peru

What does birdsong let other birds know?
How do birds learn to sing as they grow?
I wonder and ask, ask and wonder!

If you live surrounded by trees, you do not need an alarm clock to awaken you. The songs of birds at the crack of dawn can provide all the wake-up noise you need. Some birds make short calls, others longer. Some have musical songs, and others almost mechanical or raucous ones. Varied songs have earned birds names such as whooping crane; lyrebird, for its song of varied pitches; screech owl; warbler; kookaburra, whose laughter reminds the sky people to light the sun; cuckoo; mockingbird; and hoopoe. The blacksmith and coppersmith birds might be considered the "heavy metal band of the bird world," for their songs have the metallic sounds of their namesakes' work.

Birds who live in dense forests have the most piercing cries, for the thick foliage makes it difficult for these birds to see one another. Their penetrating calls enable them to know where other birds are and to communicate various kinds of information.

Flocks of birds, such as flamingos, use their calls to keep members of the flock together for protection and to warn them if danger is near. Woodpeckers combine their song with an amazing array of percussive tappings made with their beaks and feet. The chirps and tappings can convey many messages; for example, that a tree with holes in it has been found. Male birds choose a territory and fly from point to point in that territory, calling out a warning to potential intruders that they will be attacked if they trespass.

These warnings serve to establish the territory necessary for the survival of the male bird and his mate. At times, birds may be more threatened by their own kind than by birds of another species. For example, if there are too many robins in one area, there will not be enough worms to go around. By spacing themselves apart from one another, each pair of robins in its own territory, there will be plenty of worms for all. Because mockingbirds eat seeds, mockingbirds and robins can live in the same territory, for they do not threaten each other's food supply. A mockingbird will sing its warning and, if need be, attack other seed-eating birds, but it will not attack the worm-eating robins.

Birds sing warnings to keep enemies away from their nests, eggs, and young hatchlings. Usually, the male bird sings. Throughout the mating season, he sings to attract a mate. The louder and stronger the song, the more likely he is to succeed at finding a mate. The song tells the female that the potential mate will be aggressive enough to protect her and their offspring. In some species of birds, such as the European robin, the female also sings but only in wintertime. At this time, the male is not present, and the female robin must defend the territory.

The same species of bird sings the same songs. However, just as human beings' accents differ from one locale to another, so do the accents of birds! Their songs vary somewhat in sound and emphasis, depending on what geographical region they live in. Some studies of birdsong show that, although birds usually sing to defend territories, attract mates, send out warnings, and so forth, they also sing, at times, simply for pleasure.

Baby birds learn their songs from their parents through a process called imprinting. They hear their parents sing and record this song in their brains. Later, they imitate the song. If a young bird is separated from its parents, it may learn to imitate whatever bird or animal it spends most of its time near, say, a frog! Other birds, called mimic birds, copy and learn the songs of several birds. Parrots and mockingbirds do this. Parrots are also able to mimic the sound of some human words.

In the land of Peru, along the Amazon River, a legend exists about a mythical or make-believe bird called the *ayaymama.* How this bird learned its song is told in a wonderful story by the native Indians who live in the rain forest of South America. If you enter your imagination, you can travel to the village of the Yaugua Indians, who live in the Amazon along the Momon River. Picture yourself and some friends in a small wooden boat, paddling through the dense tropical foliage that fringes this river, far from modern civilization.

Look! On the white sandbanks of the river lies an Indian settlement with huts made of palm leaf roofs supported by palm trunks. How will the Yaugua people react when they see you? In the Amazon, the village chiefs make the laws. This means that, if the Indians want to capture or kill uninvited guests, it would be very difficult for the civil police to stop them.

As you pull your boat ashore, the Indians surround you and chant, "*Chi, chi, chi, chi, chi.*" Roughly translated, this is a sarcastic greeting poking fun at you and your friends. They are saying, "Look at those show-offs coming to visit us all dressed in clothing." They are also laughing, which is a good sign. To them your clothes are strange and funny. After all, living in such a hot climate, they wear only short grass skirts and seed necklaces. Their laughter indicates that, in spite of your strange clothing, they have accepted you as visitors and possibly friends. Yauguas do not joke around with those they consider enemies. Like the birds, they must defend their territory and the supply of food and water it offers them.

Look toward the jungle and you will see a group of men returning from a hunt. They are carrying blowguns. Some of these are seven to eight feet long. Through years of practice, the hunters become deadly accurate in their use of this hunting tool. They place a dart inside the blowgun. The dart has a cotton tip coated with a deadly poison called curare. The curare works only if it enters the bloodstream through a wound. If someone were to drink the poison, it most likely would have very little effect because it would go through the digestive tract and then be eliminated. That is why animals killed with curare can be eaten without harming those who eat them.

The Yaugua medicine man is a revered and respected person. His predecessors have passed down the secrets of the healing plants and herbs of the rain forests. With these, he can often cure everything from snake bite to deadly fevers, skin rashes to infections from injuries. The villagers have utter faith in his abilities. Today, scientists are seeking out the few remaining medicine men to learn their secrets of nature's garden of cures, for with the destruction of the rain forests, there will soon be no one left with this most important and valuable knowledge.

The most enjoyable time of day in the life of a Yaugua Indian is evening. This is when all the inhabitants of the village dress in their headdresses made of toucan feather and earrings made from the wings of beetles. They gather at the chief's hut to eat deer and monkey meat and tropical fruits and to tell stories, dance, and laugh. Enter your imagination and sit with the Yaugua in the chief's hut as the storyteller tells the intriguing tale of the ayaymama bird.

In Search of the Ayaymama Bird

Great Chief Coranke ruled our people many seasons ago. He wore the skin of a jaguar, for he had killed the powerful animal with his own bare hands, so great was his strength. Nara, his wife, could weave the leaves of the *shambira* palms into hammocks faster than stars twinkle in the sky. Chief Coranke and Nara had a little daughter named Raina, who also had a great gift. She loved her fellow villagers and could make everyone feel happy, no matter how sad or ill they might be. She would sing a song and do as the song said, bringing laughter to all who heard her bubbling voice:

Dun da dun ba bon, Dun da dun ba bon.
Dun da dun ba bon, Dun da dun ba bon.
I laugh all the day, I laugh all the day.
I laugh all the day, I laugh all the day.

Dun da dun ba bon, Dun da dun ba bon.
Dun da dun ba bon, Dun da dun ba bon.
Stand upon my head, Wiggle all my toes.
Stand upon my head, Wiggle all my toes.

Dun da dun ba bon, Dun da dun ba bon.
Dun da dun ba bon, Dun da dun ba bon.
Quack just like a duck, Ribbet like a frog.
Quack just like a duck, Ribbet like a frog.

Dun da dun ba bon, Dun da dun ba bon.
Dun da dun ba bon, Dun da dun ba bon.
Laughing all the day, Dun da dun ba bon!
Laughing all the day, Dun da dun ba bon!

Now, in the jungle in those times, there lived an evil spirit called Chullachaqui. He looked like a man, except that one of his feet was shaped like the hoof of a goat. Chullachaqui did not eat food. He gained his nourishment and strength from the suffering and pain of others. He was the one who caused rivers to rise and flood the land, wiping out whole villages. He was the one who sent plagues of locusts to eat the fruit trees and berry bushes. And he was the one who sent wild animals to attack the women as they gathered fruits and berries. Whenever he succeeded in causing pain and misery, Chullachaqui's cackling laugh echoed through the jungle, causing the animals to run and hide in terror.

Chullachaqui had one enemy. His enemy was Raina. No matter what evil he managed to cast on the land and its people, Raina had the power to soothe their misery and create laughter. Chullachaqui chanted like this:

Heh heh heh heh heh heh heh heh
Heh heh heh heh heh heh heh heh
Raina is stealing all the pain and sorrow.
I must stop her by tomorrow.
My evil powers are all inside the jungle.
I must lure her into the jungle.
Heh heh heh heh, awa awa heh, awa awa heh!
Heh heh heh heh, awa awa heh, awa awa heh!

One day, Chullachaqui sat on a rock at the edge of the rain forest, for he knew that Raina loved to come there and chase butterflies. His goal was to lure her away from the safety of her people and into the rain forest, where his magic would have power over her. When he saw her, he pretended to cry, though Chullachaqui had neither a heart nor tears. He knew full well that Raina could not bear to see anyone unhappy.

Raina left her butterflies and ran to him. "What is making you so sad?"

From *Day of the Moon Shadow: Tales with Ancient Answers to Scientific Questions.*
©1995. Libraries Unlimited. (800) 237-6124.

Chullachaqui lied, "No one likes me. I am crying because I'm terribly lonely. When people see me, they run away!"

"I won't run away."

Chullachaqui continued sobbing. Then he yelled, "No one visits me in the jungle!"

"I will," Raina replied.

"Can you come now?" Chullachaqui whimpered.

"OK," Raina answered, unable to bear his sad sighs.

Chullachaqui stood up, first faking a sniffle, then breaking into a smile as he saw Raina following him into the dark, dense bushes and trees. As soon as they reached Chullachaqui's den, his cackling reverberated throughout the rain forest. Loud enough for the whole village to hear, he yelped in his ugly voice, "I got her! Ha! I got her! No more will Raina steal the pain and sorrow that are rightfully mine!"

Chief Coranke, Nara, and the whole band of hunters ran into the rain forest, following the booming sounds coming from Chullachaqui's monstrous, rasping voice. They reached Chullachaqui and saw him, but Raina could be seen nowhere.

"Do not look for Raina," Chullachaqui admonished, "for you will never see her again. I have changed her into a little bird, a bird so shy that she runs from any shadow or sound. The only way the spell can be broken is if she becomes visible to human eyes—which she won't—ever!"

At that moment, a sweet, plaintive cry pierced the hearts of the villagers and all the animals in the rain forest.

Ay-ay-ma-ma
Ay-ay-ma-ma
Ay-ay-ma-ma
Ay-ay-ma-ma
Ay-ay-ma-ma

Chief Coranke and Nara knew this was the voice of their beloved daughter, now singing her song as a bird. The hunters returned to tell the sad news to the other villagers. Chief Coranke and Nara remained in the rain forest day after day, night after night, desperately calling to Raina. They hoped that, even as a bird, she would hear them and somehow remember their voices and allow them to see her, thus breaking Chullachaqui's evil spell.

Raina, in the meantime, found the nest of a newborn chick that had lost its parents. She was frightened and stayed in the nest, snuggling against the little bird while warbling her plaintive cry, "ay-ay-ma-ma." The villagers, steeped in sorrow, would answer the call. Soon, all the mimic birds of the jungle did the same. "Ay-ay-ma-ma" became a loud chant that rang throughout the jungle. Its sound irritated Chullachaqui. Day after day he grew more irritable.

One day, he could stand the sound of "ay-ay-ma-ma" no longer. He banged his head against trees, stomped his goat's hoof upon the ground, and roared, "Shut up! Shut up!" In his rage and fury, he climbed up the tree where Raina lay in the nest. With his rough, strong hands he shoved her out!

As she flew, Chief Coranke and Nara, who had remained in the rain forest all this time, hoping for a glimpse of the bird that was their daughter, saw her at last. In midair, the spell broke. Raina, no longer a bird, could not fly! She came tumbling toward the ground from the high branches of the tree. Chief Coranke leaped into the air and caught her seconds before she hit a large, jagged root.

Chief Coranke clutched Raina tightly in his arms. He and Nara ran swiftly, as animals being chased by a hungry predator must run. Chullachaqui ran close behind them, roaring louder with each step. Evil thoughts and spells with which to harm the three filled Chullachaqui's head, but in his desire to find the most evil of his spells, he forgot how near he was to the edge of the jungle. Before he could decide which spell to cast, Chief Coranke, Nara, and Raina had reached the outskirts of the jungle. Here, Chullachaqui's evil could work no more. His fury echoed throughout the jungle and beyond as he screeched and bellowed in rage.

Joy overcame everyone as they saw Chief Coranke, Nara, and Raina return to the village. They began to celebrate. Once again, as deer meat roasted and happy drums played, Raina sang her song:

> *Dun da dun ba bon, Dun da dun ba bon.*
> *Dun da dun ba bon, Dun da dun ba bon.*
> *Stand upon my head, Wiggle all my toes.*
> *Stand upon my head, Wiggle all my toes.*
>
> *Dun da dun ba bon, Dun da dun ba bon.*
> *Dun da dun ba bon, Dun da dun ba bon.*
> *Quack just like a duck, Ribbet like a frog.*
> *Quack just like a duck, Ribbet like a frog.*
>
> *Dun da dun ba bon, Dun da dun ba bon.*
> *Dun da dun ba bon, Dun da dun ba bon.*
> *Laughing all the day, Dun da dun ba bon!*
> *Laughing all the day, Dun da dun ba bon!*

Suddenly, amid the happy noise of the festivities, a cry was heard from deep within the jungle:

Ay-ay-ma-ma.
Ay-ay-ma-ma.

The little bird whom Raina had befriended when she was a bird had become imprinted with Raina's song, "ay-ay-ma-ma!" Forever after and to this day, it is said that the ayaymama bird can be heard singing throughout the rain forest. As for Chullachaqui, he could stand it no longer. He ran to the banks of the Momon River, dived in, hid under a rock, and plugged up his ears with mud. He has never bothered the Yaugua again!

References

Science

- Burton, Maurice. 1985. *The World of Science: Birds*. New York: Facts on File.

- Line, Les. 1993. "Silence of the Songbirds." *National Geographic* 183, no. 6 (June).

- Perrins, Christopher M., and Alex L. A. Middleton, eds. 1985. *The Encyclopedia of Birds*. New York: Facts on File.

- Peterson, Rodger Tory. 1963. *The Birds*. New York: Life Science Library.

- Tinbergen, Niko. 1965. *Animal Behavior*. New York: Life Nature Library.

Anthropology

- Chagnon, Napoleon A. 1938. *Yanomamo: The Fierce People*, 3d ed. New York: Holt, Rinehart & Winston.

- Cowell, Adrian. 1960. *The Heart of the Forest*. New York: Alfred A. Knopf.

- Fejos, Paul. 1943. *Ethnography of the Yaugua*. New York: Viking.

- Llosa, Mario Vargas. 1989. *The Storyteller*. New York: Penguin Books.

- Plotkin, Mark J. 1993. *Tales of a Shaman's Apprentice*. New York: Penguin Books.

- Weaver, Kenneth F. 1964. "The Five Worlds of Peru." *National Geographic* 125, no. 2 (February).

- *Webster's New International Dictionary*. 1921. G. & C. Merriam.

Folklore

- Campbell, Joseph. 1989. *Historical Atlas of World Mythology*. New York: Harper & Row.

- Llosa, Mario Vargas. 1989. *The Storyteller*. New York: Penguin Books.

- Rugoff, Milton, ed. 1949. *A Harvest of World Folktales*. New York: Viking. ("In Search of the Ayaymama Bird" was inspired by the traditional tale "Ayaymama" found in this source.)

- Willis, Roy. 1993. *World Mythology*. New York: Henry Holt.

Music

- *Indian Music of the Upper Amazon*. Folkways 4458.

- *The Music of Primitive Colombians*. Columbia Records.

- *The Pelicour Indians of the Arcua River in Brazil*. Folkways 4236.

Raina's Happy Song

From "In Search of the Ayaymama Bird"

Music and Lyrics by
JUDY GAIL

Chullachaqui's Problem

From "In Search of the Ayaymama Bird"

Music and Lyrics by
JUDY GAIL

Ayaymama

From "In Search of the Ayaymama Bird"
Page 1

Music and Lyrics by
JUDY GAIL

cue: In fact, it became a chant that was
heard day and night...

cue: Chullachaqui covered his ears and yelled...

Ayaymama

From "In Search of the Ayaymama Bird"
Page 2

Percussion continues through narration.

cue: Suddenly, in a
fit of insane rage...

Voice stops

Ay- ay- ma- ma

cue: ...and caught Raina inches
above the ground.

24

cue: Suddenly, all talking
and laughing stopped.

cue: Chullachaqui listened.

cue: The little bird...

Ay- ay- ma- ma.

Ay- ay- ma-

cue: Forever after and to this day, it is said

ma.

that the *ayaymama* bird can be heard singing throughout the rain forest.

4

The Khevsouri and the Cure

THE KHEVSOURI AND THE CURE

A Story from the Georgian Mountains of Russia

Why do colds make us sneeze?
How does a doctor's shot cure a disease?
I wonder and ask, ask and wonder!

Compare the blood flowing through your body to a peaceful, harmonious river. It starts out at the pumping station—*Heart*ville. Then it flows on through *Stomach*ville, *Liver*ville, *Kidney*ville, *Brain*ville, even *Skin*ville! It flows to and through every organ in your body, carrying vitamins, nutrients, minerals, all the nourishment needed to keep you alive, healthy, and well. Yes, everything is pleasant, in harmony, functioning perfectly.

Suddenly, you get a stomachache, headache, sore throat, earache, fever, and chills. The Alien Invaders have come—germs, bacteria, viruses! Aha! Your blood's own built-in army—antibodies ("anti" means "against")—comes to the rescue! The antibodies fight the Alien Invaders and make it impossible for them to survive. The antibodies damage these invaders so that they cannot live in your blood, destroy your cells, and take away the nourishment meant for you.

Most of the time, the antibodies are the victors and win the battle. Every now and then, however, the antibodies have difficulty fighting the battle alone. A bacterial infection or a virus is sometimes too virulent for them. That is when, thanks to modern medicines, we can call in the marines—the doctor's shot! Ouch! Why must we get hurt in order to get better? The answer is that, in this shot, is a medical discovery called antibiotics. Antibiotics attack bacteria and destroy them so that they cannot function or fight back. The antibiotics help our antibodies in their battle against the Alien Invaders.

Another type of shot is called a vaccination. In a vaccination against diseases like measles, whooping cough, and smallpox, weakened or dead viruses are injected into the bloodstream. Immediately, this invasion sets the antibodies into action, and they go to war against the invaders. Because the vaccination contains weakened or dead bacteria or viruses, the antibodies automatically win. Now, because the antibodies are already in action, if really strong bacteria or viruses try to enter the bloodstream, they cannot even get past the cannon's roar—they cannot even begin to fight. The antibodies are so ready for that first cannon blast, that first attack, that the invaders die before firing even one shot.

Many diseases that once killed millions of people around the world, such as rheumatic fever, polio, smallpox, diphtheria, scarlet fever, and whooping cough— diseases often caught by young children—have been eliminated, curtailed, or otherwise brought under control because of the development of antibiotics and vaccinations.

Hundreds of years ago, and even as early as the beginning of the 20th century, knowledge of antibiotics and other modern medicines did not exist. Yet, people got sick and had to cure themselves. In a valley hidden in the Georgian Mountains of southwestern Russia, the people of past centuries and still some in this century lived to be much older than anyone living today—without the help of modern medicines. It was not unusual to see a 101-year-old man threshing wheat on his farm, or a 120-year-old woman weaving a carpet on a loom. In 1973, a woman from the Georgian Mountains named Mrs. Lazuria celebrated her 141st birthday! How did she and the other people in her region live to be so old and fight off diseases without the aid of modern medicines?

When asked about this, Mrs. Lazuria and her fellow Georgians explained that their people know of many amazing healing plants that grow in the garden of earth and how to use these plants to keep their bodies in tune with nature. "In these mountains," they said, "we learn how to listen to our bodies. If our bodies say, 'I'm tired,' or 'I don't feel well,' we don't just take an aspirin and keep on working. We go and rest until our bodies say, 'OK, I feel like working again!'" They explained that it is hard for our bodies to keep going when they do not feel well, and that pain is just the way our bodies tell us, "I need a break!" If our bodies are tired or weakened, our army of antibodies will not be able to fight off Alien Invaders as effectively and efficiently.

They also recommended fibrous, whole-grain bread made from wheat like that grown on their farms, instead of bread bought in grocery stores today, from which many of the nutrients and natural fibers are removed and chemicals added to soften and preserve it. They also suggested drinking a glass of fermented goat's milk daily. Mrs. Lazuria added, "If you are going to get married, a woman should find a nice husband, and a man, a nice wife, because nothing will make you grow old faster than a nagging, nasty mate!" Her biggest secret to a long and healthy life was "Live with love and love to live!"

Imagine visiting the Georgian Mountains 100, 200, or 500 years ago, before modern medicine. Enter a town called Khevsoureti. The townspeople here are called Khevsouris. You see white houses with quaint, small windows, and each house is three stories high. Each has a watch tower at the top because Turks, Muslims, and Russian czars frequently attack and try to take over the valley. Even the centenarians, people over 100 years of age, are on guard and strong fighters when they must battle. The Khevsouris wear sharp, double-edged daggers on their belts. The boys and girls wear embroidered shirts called *chokhas*. In the dialect spoken here, *ara* means "yes," and *ki* means "no." While fighting off enemies, you can hear the hardy Khevsouris yelling, *"Ki! Ki! Ki!"* as they brandish their swords and daggers.

The farms are filled with goats, sheep, and fields of wheat and barley. The mountains are covered with wild flowers and herbs, mosses and trees. The Khevsouris know much about how to use plants and tree barks to make teas, decoctions, ointments, and other natural medicines to stay healthy and to cure themselves when they are sick. These people have their own beliefs about what causes illness, and, of course, their own cures. For example, they believe that garlic both prevents and cures many illnesses. Heads of garlic hang at the doorways of houses, and the Khevsouris wear garlic cloves on a string as necklaces. The garlic, it is believed, also wards off evil.

The Khevsouris also believe in a devil called the Eshmahkie. The Eshmahkie loves nothing more than to steal the secrets of cures away from the memories of those who know how to cure. The Eshmahkie relishes the confusion and illness he causes by doing this.

Almost everyone here tells stories. With so many years of life lived and still to live, there are many stories to tell. Imagine yourself sitting at the wooden table in the kitchen of a Khevsouri. A fire burns in the hearth. A balalaika, a three-stringed musical instrument, hangs on the wall. Heads of garlic, their tops braided together, surround you as they hang from the ceiling, and shelves are filled with dried herbs—dandelions, violets, lemon grass, and more. The Khevsouri, a robust man with a deep voice and a thick mustache, tells you the tale of two centenarians—Georgi and Tinatin Gigauri.

The Khevsouri and the Cure

Georgi Gigauri and his wife, Tinatin, lived in their house on their farm. Georgi, because he lived in Khevsoureti, was called the Khevsouri. Every day, he and Tinatin went to sleep with the moonlight and woke up with the sunlight. They sat down to eat their breakfast of delicious, fibrous bread, *gudis khveli*, which is a pungent cheese made from sheep's milk, and, of course, drink their glass of fermented goat's milk. Happily, they sang

> *Roosters crow and herbs grow on our farm in Khevsoureti!*
> *Honey flows and flowers grow right here in Khevsoureti!*
> *Georgi Gigauri, Tinatin Gigauri, Zviade Gigauri!*
> *Here's to our life in Khevsoureti HEY!*

Georgi and Tinatin were each 101 years old. They had children, grand-children, great-grandchildren, and great-great-grandchildren. Today they were particularly happy because their great-great-grandson, six-year-old Zviade, was to spend the harvest holiday with them. After the Khevsouri finished his day of cutting wheat in his wheat fields, he returned to the farmhouse just in time to hear the rumbling of wooden wheels on the mountain road and the whinnying of a horse.

"Zviade!" the Khevsouri cried. "Zviade is here!" He and Tinatin ran outside, and sure enough, little Zviade arrived in the horse-drawn cart that had carried him to Khevsoureti from his mountain village some 40 miles away. Georgi lifted his great-great-grandson up and gave him a big hug and kiss. Then they all went into the house, and Zviade did his favorite thing of all things to do. He sat on his great-great-grandfather's knee and listened to stories of 101 years of life and to their special little song.

> *Way back when I was just a little boy,*
> *My brothers and my sisters and my father and my mother*
> *Would work in the sun, play games in the rain,*
> *We all had work to do, but we never did complain.*
> *We had fun at what we did. We did not have to make choices,*
> *And when we were through, we danced to our own voices,*
> *Or the music of the birds, or the breath of life we breathed.*
> *Yes, here's to the simple life, it's all that you should need!*
> *Yes, here's to the simple life, it's all that you should need!*

The next morning, Zviade helped his great-great-grandmother feed the animals. The Khevsouri, as he did each day, picked up his sharp scythe with its long wooden handle and went to the wheat fields to cut more grain. A gentle breeze whispered through the wheat. Then, without warning, a forceful gust of wind blew in. It was a very strange gust, for it did not sway or bend the grass or trees—not even ruffle the hairs that still grew on the Khevsouri's head. The only thing the wind blew was—garlic! From everywhere, fresh cloves of garlic came whirling through the air like locusts in swarms. The cloves blew until they flew right off the Gigauri farm. Then, as quickly as the wind had started, it stopped! The Khevsouri felt frightened and bewildered.

Something strange is happening right here.
It feels a little bad and it feels a little queer.
Yes, something strange is happening right here!
Na na na na na na na-a na na.

Always here upon the Gigauri farm,
We've been free from sickness,
Free from fear and harm.
Love and happiness have been our magic charm.
Na na na na na na na-a na na.

Why now do I feel this reeling in my head,
And want not to be working but to lie down in my bed?
I seem to be forgetting things. What is it I just said?
Na na na na na na na-a na na.
Na na na na na na na-a na na.

The Khevsouri picked up his scythe and cut wheat. He cut one stalk—whishooh! He cut two stalks—whishooh! He cut three stalks—whishooh! For each swing of his scythe, he heard another swing. For each stalk he cut, he saw another stalk fall. He turned around and there, on his farm, right before his own eyes, was the Eshmahkie—the little devil himself! "Why are you here?" Georgi asked.

"Why are you here?" the Eshmahkie mocked him.

"I asked you! Why are you here?"

"I asked you! Why are you here?" the Eshmahkie imitated him again.

"Answer me!" demanded the Khevsouri.

"Answer me!" came the Eshmahkie's response.

"Oh, stop imitating me!"

"Oh, stop imitating me!" The Eshmahkie taunted the Khevsouri further by singing

Click, click, click! Hiss, hiss hiss!
Please give the Eshmahkie one great big kiss.
Kiss the devil, even hug him if you dare.
Dare the devil, for the devil may care!

"*Ki!*" shouted Georgi. "*Ki!*" He was so infuriated that he bit his tongue to prevent himself from talking further to the Eshmahkie. Instead, he took his sharp scythe and cut several stalks of wheat. He wound them into a taut, tight twine, sat down, tied his feet together, and put his sharp scythe by his side. The Eshmahkie imitated him. He cut several stalks of wheat with a stick, wound them into a taut, tight twine, sat down, tied his feet together, and put his dull stick by his side.

From *Day of the Moon Shadow: Tales with Ancient Answers to Scientific Questions.*
©1995. Libraries Unlimited. (800) 237-6124.

The Khevsouri now took his sharp scythe, cut the twine between his feet, and stood up. The Eshmahkie, imitating him, took his dull stick and tried to cut the twine between his feet, but the dull stick would not cut through the twine. "Get me out of here! Get me out of here!" he begged. "Out! Out! Out! Just show me you care, and I promise I'll leave you alone!"

"I've heard about you, Eshmahkie. You make promises, and then you break promises!"

"You make promises, and then you break promises!" the Eshmahkie imitated.

The Khevsouri was so angry, he picked up his scythe and walked toward home, leaving the Eshmahkie sitting in the wheat field with his feet tied together. As the Khevsouri approached the house, he saw Tinatin running across the field, waving her hands. Tears ran down her face. "Georgi, Georgi," she cried. "A big gust of wind blew through the house. It blew my necklace of garlic right off my neck. It blew the braids of garlic right off the ceiling. Little Zviade lies in bed sick with high fever! What should I do? What should I do?"

"Tinatin, you know what to do! You are an expert at knowing how to cure fever!"

"But, Georgi, I don't remember anything. I can't even remember what garlic is for!"

When the Khevsouri thought about this, he realized he could not remember what garlic was for either! "Tinatin, we are only 101 years old. This is too young to be losing our memories!" But the only thing either of them could remember was to hold each other's hands and walk to their house. When they arrived, Georgi went to the bed where little Zviade lay, redder than the reddest beet in the whole world! He touched the child's head, and the heat of the fever burned the tips of his fingers. "Zviade, Zviade, open your eyes!" Georgi cried. "Look at great-great-grandpa! Talk to me!" But Zviade was too sick to open his eyes or speak. Tinatin cried and sighed.

What, oh what, oh what will we do?
Zviade, we don't know what to do with you.
There you lie so sick that you could die,
And all we remember is how to cry.

From *Day of the Moon Shadow: Tales with Ancient Answers to Scientific Questions*.
©1995. Libraries Unlimited. (800) 237-6124.

Tears roll down our cheeks from our eyes.
Our ears only hear your delirious sighs.
With all of the cures that grow on our land,
We remember none, as though our heads were filled with sand.
Ay ay ay ay ay ay Zviade, Zviade.

"Oh, Georgi, it is as though the Eshmahkie were right here casting his spell upon us!"

When Georgi heard the word Eshmahkie, he did not know whether he was awake or asleep, imagining or dreaming, but his legs began to run under him—fast, then faster—and even faster. His legs moved as though they had a life of their own! They took him to the wheat fields. There, he saw the truth before his eyes, as he gazed at the Eshmahkie, still sitting with his feet tied together and the dull stick by his side.

Don't play with the devil, for Eshmahkie may dare
To kill little Zviade, and even eat his hair!
I might change my mind if your scythe will tear
This rope-like twine and get my feet out of here!

"Get me out! Get me out!" the Eshmahkie screeched.

"I will cut the twine," Georgi replied, "but first you must answer a question of mine!"

"You cut the twine, and then I'll answer your question!"

"I don't trust you!"

"I don't trust you!"

"Stop imitating me!"

"I'm not imitating you. I really don't trust you!" The Eshmahkie was exasperated. "We both mistrust each other, and we certainly don't think alike!"

"You answer my question, and then I'll cut the twine!" Georgi insisted.

"You cut the twine, and then I'll answer your question!" the Eshmahkie persisted.

"*KI!*" roared Georgi.

"*ARA!*" the Eshmahkie shrieked.

"*KI!*"

"ARA!"

"KI!"

"ARA!"

"KIIIIIIII!" The Khevsouri was ready to explode when, in his mind's eye, he saw the image of little Zviade lying redder than the reddest beet in the whole world, sick with fever. He knew the child's life came first and foremost. It could not be sacrificed for a battle of wills, mistrust, and power. He picked up his scythe and cut the twine between the Eshmahkie's feet. The Eshmahkie jumped up and ran!

"Wait! Wait!" The Khevsouri screamed. "You promised to answer my question!"

"What makes you think an Eshmahkie keeps his promises?"

"Well, Eshmahkie, when I tied my feet together with the twine, I knew you would imitate me and that your dull stick would not be able to cut as my sharp scythe can. I thought I would outsmart you and put an end to your evil forever."

"And then, I outsmarted you, Khevsouri, because, even with my feet tied together, I was able to cast an evil spell on you and cause illness in little Zviade and rob even your Tinatin's memory of the secret of cures!"

"Well, Eshmahkie, that is my question! How can illness be cured?"

"To show you that there are no hard feelings between us, Khevsouri, I will answer you. To cure fever, you make the patient even hotter. For snake bite, you administer snake venom. If a person eats a poison berry, you give another poison to make the body eliminate the first poison. Remember now? The secret to curing illness is to give a little less of what caused the illness to begin with! Good-bye!"

"Good-bye!"

"Stop imitating me!" the Eshmahkie mocked as he disappeared.

The Khevsouri ran home. He went into the house. "Tinatin, Tinatin! The secret to curing illness is to give a little less of what caused the illness to begin with!"

When Tinatin heard this, her eyes lit up like all the stars over the mountaintops at night. Her joy increased as the garlic, which had so suddenly blown away, all blew back just as suddenly. She ran from jar to jar, jug to jug, mixing concoctions and decoctions. She placed little Zviade on a cold towel and then wrapped two hot towels around him. She covered him with a quilt filled with goose feathers to make him even hotter so he could sweat out the fever and the toxins in his body. She boiled water and made a tonic from dandelions—a fortifying tonic guaranteed to give him strength. She boiled the flowers of violets and then strained the water and gave it to Zviade to drink in order to relieve his aches and pains and calm his nerves. Then she made him a broth of water, fresh garlic, lemon juice, and honey—the honey not only for sweetness but because it was known to cure over 100 different ailments!

It wasn't but three days until little Zviade was sitting up and talking to his great-great-grandparents. By the end of the week, he was all better—just in time for the harvest holiday. Once again he did his favorite thing of all things to do. He sat on his great-great-grandfather's knee and listened to stories of 101 years of life!

On this night, the Khevsouri said, "Zviade, in life there is good and evil, happiness and sorrow, sickness and health. If we open ourselves to the garden of earth, we can find joy—and an answer and a cure for all things. Yes, my little Zviade," and he sang

Roosters crow and wheat grows on our farm in Khevsoureti!
Cabbage sprouts and goats baa on our farm in Khevsoureti!
Georgi Gigauri, Tinatin Gigauri, Zviade Gigauri!
Here's to our life in Khevsoureti HEY!

References

Science

- Carter, Richard. 1966. *Breakthrough: The Saga of Jonas Salk*. New York: Trident Press.

- Culpeper, Nicholas. 1985. *Culpeper's Complete Herbal*. Secaucus, NJ: Chartwell.

- Duke, James A. 1985. *CRC Handbook of Medicinal Herbs*. Boca Raton, FL: CRC Press.

- Harre, Rom. 1981. *Great Scientific Experiments*. Oxford: Phaidon Press.

- Irvin, George W., ed. 1949. *Antibiotics*. Brooklyn, NY: Chemical.

- Shelton, Ferne 1965. *Pioneer Comforts and Kitchen Remedies—Old Timey Highland Secrets from the Blue Ridge and Great Smokey Mountains*. High Point, NC: Hutcraft.

- Shurkin, Joel N. 1979. *The Invisible Fire: The Story of Mankind's Victory over the Ancient Scurge of Smallpox*. New York: Putnam.

- Welch, Henry. 1953. *Antibiotic Therapy*. New York: Medical Encyclopedia.

Anthropology

- Dolphin, Laurie. 1991. *Georgia to Georgia: Making Friends in the USSR*. New York: Tambourine Books.

- Goldstein, Darra. 1993. *Georgian Feast—The Vibrant Culture and Savory Food of the Republic of Georgia*. New York: HarperCollins.

- Leaf, Alexander. 1973. "Everyday Is a Gift When You Are over 100." *National Geographic* 143, no. 1 (January).

- McDowell, Bart. 1977. *Journey Across Russia: The Soviet Union Today*. Washington, DC: National Geographic Society.

- *Russian Photographic Portrait*. n.d. New York: Crescent Books.

Folklore

- Downing, Charles, reteller. 1989. *Russian Tales and Legends*. Oxford: Oxford University Press.

- Rugoff, Milton, ed. 1949. *A Harvest of World Folktales*. New York: Viking Press. ("The Khevsouri and the Cure" was inspired by the traditional tale "The Khevsouri and the Eshmahkie" as found in this source.)

Music

- *Folkmusic of the USSR*. Folkways, 4535 AB, 4535 CD.

- *Music of the Georgian Mountains*. An audiocassette prepared by Mr. David Chikzaidze, cultural attaché of the Soviet embassy, displaying a mixture of songs and melodies from the Georgian Mountains.

Our Farm in Khevsoureti

From "The Khevsouri and the Cure"

Music and Lyrics by
JUDY GAIL

Verse one is sung at the beginning of the story, verse two at the end.

When I Was Just a Little Boy

From "The Khevsouri and the Cure"

Music and Lyrics by
JUDY GAIL

This song sounds particularly nice with the accompaniment of guitar and flute.

Something Strange

From "The Khevsouri and the Cure"
Page 1

Music and Lyrics by
JUDY GAIL

This song sounds good accompanied by guitar and accoustic bass or similar sound on keyboard.

Something Strange

From "The Khevsouri and the Cure"
Page 2

been our mag- ic charm. Na na na na na na na - a na

na. Why now do I feel this

reel- ing in my head, and want not to be work- ing but to

lie down in my bed? I seem to be for- get- ing things. What

is it I just said? Na na na na na na na - a na

na. Na na na na na na na - a na na.

Song of the Eshmahkie

From "The Khevsouri and the Cure"

Music and Lyrics by
JUDY GAIL

This song may be accompanied by guitar, piano, balalaika, or an electronic keyboard sound of your own choosing.

What Will We Do?

From "The Khevsouri and the Cure"
Page 1

Music and Lyrics by
JUDY GAIL

What, — oh what, — oh what will we do? _____

_____ Zvi- a- de, we don't know what to do with

you. _____ There you _____ lie so sick that you could

die, and all we re- mem- ber is how _____ to

cry.

Tears roll _____ down our cheeks from our eyes. _____ Our

What Will We Do?

From "The Khevsouri and the Cure"
Page 2

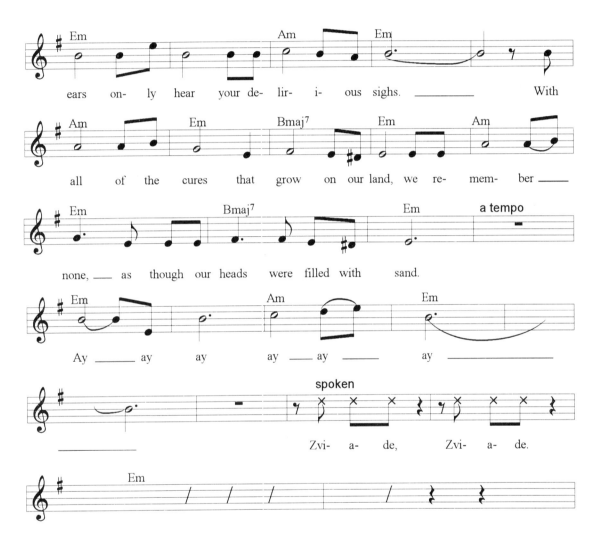

A guitar and a violin, either real or simulated on an electronic keyboard, would be a nice accompaniment for this song.

The Eshmahkie's Threat

From "The Khevsouri and the Cure"

Music and Lyrics by
JUDY GAIL

Don't play with the de-- vil, for Esh- mah- kie may dare

to kill Zvi- a- de and ev- en eat his hair!

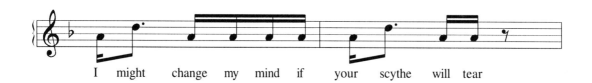

I might change my mind if your scythe will tear

this rope- like twine and get my feet out of here! ————

Use the same accompaniment here as for the first "Song of the Eshmahkie."

5
MONSTERS OF THE SKY LAND

Monsters of the Sky Land

A Story from the Dieri Tribe of the Aborigines of Australia

Why did all the dinosaurs die?
What created the desert and sky?
I wonder and ask, ask and wonder!

Paleontologists are scientists who study prehistoric life forms through the careful examination of fossil plants and animals. Fossils are remnants of a past geological age, such as a skeleton, footprint, leaf, or animal imprint embedded in earth or rocks. Over millions of years, bones, teeth, shells, wood, and other materials can become fossilized if the right conditions exist. Minerals, usually from water, slowly replace the dead organic, or once-living, material. Drop by drop, cell by cell, the minerals seep in and slowly crystallize, most often in the exact shape of the original organic object, leaving it hardened like stone.

Paleontologists are experts at identifying fossils. They have studied the anatomy—the bone and muscle structures—of thousands of species of animals. They compare these with those in fossil bones. They know what bone would be a part of a backbone, which would be a shoulder, leg, or toe bone, even if they have never seen the animal before. For example, they can tell if a large fossilized bone is the jawbone of a whale, a woolly mammoth, or an elephant, or if it is the rib of the dinosaur triceratops or leg bone of tyrannosaurus rex. The shapes of fossilized teeth tell these scientists whether an animal was a meat-eating carnivore or a plant-eating herbivore. Studying fossilized feces, or droppings of animals long gone, they can tell what the animal ate and even what bacteria existed in that animal's lifetime.

Our earth is estimated to be 4.6 billion years old. Do you know, however, that dinosaurs were not truly discovered, that is put together and scientifically studied, until less than 200 years ago? In 1822, a woman named Mary Mantell found an enormous tooth in a rock quarry. She showed it to her husband, Dr. Gideon Mantell, who was a naturalist, a scientist knowledgeable in natural history, especially zoology and botany.

Dr. Mantell, who became one of the first recognized paleontologists, suspected that the tooth belonged to an unknown animal. After several years of comparing this tooth with others, he discovered that it was similar to the teeth of an iguana. He and other scientists returned to the area where the strange tooth had been found and unearthed more fossils, including a jawbone into which this large tooth fit! The bones were huge—in fact, gigantic!

It took many years, as it takes all paleontologists, for Dr. Mantell and his colleagues to piece together this skeleton. These are extremely difficult and complicated puzzles to reconstruct, for some bones are missing, and others must be matched with some similar existing animal's skeletal structure as a clue to how to put them together. Finally, when they did put the bones together, iguanodon, a genuine dinosaur, was reconstructed! They named it "iguanodon," from the Arawak word for lizard and the Greek root word, *odon,* for tooth. The paleontologists knew which muscles, sinews, and ligaments went over specific kinds of bones. Because of this, they were able to draw a picture of what a living iguanodon might have looked like.

After this, scientists around the world became convinced that there must have been more such creatures. They dug from one end of the world to the other and found more bones—enormous bones. When the puzzle pieces were put together, they named these creatures "dinosaurs," which means "terrible lizards" in Greek. They proceeded to find stegosaurus, apatosaurus, brachiosaurus, triceratops, tyrannosaurus rex—and they continue to find more today, such as ultrasaurus and mononychus, a new link between dinosaurs and birds! These scientists, through various tests, could tell that the dinosaurs lived some 300 million years ago and died out, or became extinct, only 65 million years ago. Why? What happened?

There are many theories, both religious and scientific, about what might have caused this extinction, from a great flood to a huge meteor colliding with the earth and creating such a cloud of dust that the sun's rays could not penetrate it and warm the earth for animals and plants to live. We do not know for sure, and perhaps we never will. However, thanks to the paleontologists, we know a tremendous amount about dinosaurs. Before paleontologists discovered and gave us this fascinating information, what did people think when they found monster-sized bones?

Long, long ago, when people first began to make tools, they frequently used bones for these tools and other objects. Bones could be used to cut or spear. They could be made into necklaces or chewed for calcium. The oldest known flute was made from a bone. The native people of the island continent of Australia, whom we call the Aborigines, were experts at using bones, for the desert where many of them lived contained numerous bones from animals who died on the arid land.

Though surrounded by water, Australia's interior is filled with some of the most uninhabitable desert in the world. Yet the Aborigines have been able to survive there. So have many unique animals that are found nowhere else. There are the kangaroo, the koala, and one of the strangest animals in the entire world—the platypus. This animal has fur and suckles its young with milk like a mammal. It has a bill and webbed feet and lays eggs like a duck. The males have a venom gland on their hind legs that allows them to strike and poison their enemies like a venomous snake. Australians call the platypus the "bits and pieces" animal.

After Captain Cook sailed to Australia some 200 years ago and claimed it as a British colony, Australia, like England, grew into a modern country along its coastal regions. In the middle of the continent, however, where the hot, dry desert has taken the lives of many non-Aboriginal people attempting to cross it, some Aborigines live as they have for thousands and thousands of years. These Aborigines still live in a Stone Age culture. This means they acquire all their food by hunting animals and gathering wild plants. Hunting is very difficult, for on this arid land, you cannot find many animals. Aborigines know this harsh environment and how to thoroughly use whatever meager resources it has to offer. You would be amazed at what they eat and how they are able to find water to drink.

Once in a while, hunters are lucky enough to hunt and catch a kangaroo, which supplies protein, fat, and calcium sucked from the bones. Most of the time they eat lizards, often raw, for the blood affords liquid, protein, minerals, and vitamins. They also collect witchity grubs, white fat worms that they eat after roasting them on a fire. They are said to taste somewhat like pork rind. Witchity grubs are a constant supply of fat for the Aboriginal diet. In order to get sugar and carbohydrates, also necessary for survival, they dig up ants. These ants are found only in Australia and have large stomachs filled with a sweet liquid that tastes like honey. These ants are the Aborigines' candy. For starch, the Aborigines know which plants are tubers—plants that have edible, bulbous roots—and dig these up and eat them, sometimes cooked over a fire but often raw. Cactus plants, called succulents, have their own water supply in their root systems. The Aborigines know which cacti have this water supply, and this is the water they drink to survive.

The Aborigines hunt with spears and boomerangs. The boomerang is shaped so that, when thrown, it comes back to the thrower unless an animal has been hit with it. In the desert, energy must be spared. An Aborigine will run only when he is sure the animal has been hit. This clever hunting tool tells the hunter when to run and when not to run.

When Aborigines find a dinosaur bone, they wonder what creature it belonged to and why they never see that creature alive. They have a word for these unknown monsters—*kadimakara*—which, ironically, means the same thing as the word dinosaur—terrible lizard! Without any scientific knowledge but by observing only the bones, they, too, surmised what dinosaurs would have looked like alive. They came up with their own ideas about where the dinosaurs came from and why they are now extinct.

Imagine yourself on the desert of central Australia with the Dieri tribe of Aborigines. Their musicians are blowing rhythmically into their didjeridoos, instruments made from hollowed-out branches of varying sizes. Accompanying the didjeridoo players, others bang stones together and shake rattles made from twigs, dried gourds, and pebbles. The storyteller, Wingarooloo, is about to tell their legend of the *kadimakara*—the Monsters of the Sky Land.

Monsters of the Sky Land

The children of my tribe have asked, "What is the sky made of?" You ask, "What does the sky have to do with huge bones?" I answer, "Everything!" To learn about bones, we must first ask, "What is the sky made of?" Think, my children, think, then I shall tell you.

The sky is a big hole of nothing,
No earth and no water.
The sky is a spirit of darkness
And then one of light.
The sky is an empty piece of wood
That ev'rything sits upon.
The sky was filled with monstrous creatures,
But the monstrous creatures are gone!

Many, many years ago, years and years and years ago, too many moons gone by to make marks in the sand to count, the sky was held up by three very large gum trees. The trees were taller, much taller, than any gum trees today, and wider, much, much wider. The leaves on the gum trees were like giants, shading the earth from the heat of the sky. The gum nuts on the trees were, each of them, bigger, much bigger, than the whole dry desert on which we live. They had to be. Yes, my children, they had to be!

For on these gum trees in the land of the sky, there lived enormous, fierce-looking, monstrous animals. They are too big for us to even think about or imagine. They had mouths so large that they could bite the gum nuts in one bite. They had to do this, for they had to eat a lot of gum nuts in order to keep themselves alive. Some of them ate other monsters. When this happened, their fights were so great that the gum trees would bend and stretch and cause our earth to tremble and shake! Their tears of pain would pour down on our earth and fill rivers and streams, even the oceans.

These monsters were called *kadimakara*! Imagine, my children, a sand monitor lizard, a crocodile, a platypus, or a kangaroo being bigger—so big that, from where we sit now, you could not see the end of their bodies, for from the head to the end, they were too far away. Imagine, my children, a monster so enormous that the boomerang the hunters threw at it would only appear as a speck of sand in the desert on one of their bodies. It is said that

---

these huge animals roared and growled, hissed and howled, and when they did this all at once, the earth would vibrate with thunderous sounds! Chant with me now, my children, and repeat after me as we sing the song of the *kadimakara*!

Leader:
Ka
Dim
A
Kara!
Kadimakara!
Kadimakara!
Monsters!
Monsters!

Response:
Ka
Dim
A
Kara!
Kadimakara!
Kadimakara!
Monsters!
Monsters!

Leader:	Response:
In the sky!	In the sky!
In the sky!	In the sky!
Sitting,	Sitting,
Sitting	Sitting
On gum trees,	On gum trees,
On gum trees,	On gum trees,
Eating,	Eating,
Eating	Eating
Gum nuts,	Gum nuts,
Gum nuts!	Gum nuts!
Ka	Ka
Dim	Dim
A	A
Kara!	Kara!
Kadimakara!	*Kadimakara!*
Kadimakara!	*Kadimakara!*
Kadimakara! (all together)	

You are frightened by the thought of such giant beasts, aren't you? "Are the *kadimakara* still here?" I hear you ask. The answer lies in the sky! Yes, the monsters lived in the land in the sky. They walked on the tops of the gigantic gum trees and sat on the leaves and branches. They also spent much time looking down on our earth, which then was large and flat. Our earth was filled with beautiful blue waters—oceans, rivers, lakes. It had high mountains covered with delicious green grass and trees. There were lush fields and forests. The smell of eucalyptus and the hundreds of perfumed flowers traveled up to the noses of the monsters. They envied such delicious odors.

Some of the *kadimakara* flew or glided and looked like enormous birds or bats. They looked on our earth and heard the beautiful song of the lyrebird and the laughter of the kookaburra. They saw the vivid colors and graceful flight of the rainbow lorakeet—and they were jealous! They wished to be smaller like the kangaroos and to hop like kangaroos instead of walking so clumsily and slowly as their gigantic size made them walk. Yes, down here, we had beauty.

Down here we had beauty.
Earth was rich with flowers.
Earth was rich with rivers.
Earth heard the songs of the birds.
Down here we had beauty.
Earth was rich with kangaroos.
Earth was rich with night and day.
Time to hunt and time to play,
Down here, down here, down here.

Then why do we now live on a desert so dry? You don't see water or flowers or hear songbirds here where we live. We eat witchity grubs and lizards and bite the bellies of the honey ants. You want to know why the *kadimakara* saw such beautiful things here and we don't? The answer lies in the sky!

Every day, the monsters looked down on earth. Every day, there were new monsters being hatched from eggs or born alive. One day, a special monster was born, a very special *kadimakara* indeed! It was in the family of *kadimakara* that the other people call apatosaurus. This kind of *kadimakara* grows to be very huge. Why, its tail alone can reach up to 40 feet long and its weight can reach 8,000 pounds or more! But for some reason, this newborn baby apatosaurus did not grow as quickly or as big as the others. All of the monsters teased this poor little apatosaurus, who came to be known by the name Kirimumba. They laughed at Kirimumba night and day. The meat-eating dinosaurs would not think of touching Kirimumba for fear that they would be laughed at for hunting such a small meal!

Kirimumba was happy about that, for he felt safe. Kirimumba thought the land in the sky was beautiful. The leaves of the gum trees felt so pleasant under his feet, and Kirimumba loved the taste of the gum nuts. He felt no need to look down on the earth. But the other monsters bent and stretched their necks to view the earth below, and the branches of the gum trees swayed and bent more each day under their heavy weight. From the earth itself, the sound of branches cracking could be heard. Kirimumba watched the others and saw what they were doing to the trees. He was frightened and worried as he heard one branch after another begin to crackle and crack. He pleaded with the others

You will break the branches,
Listen to me!
Put away your jealousy.
Forget the earth and its greenery.
I am Kirimumba, listen to me!

The monsters only laughed at Kirimumba. The more he pleaded with them, the more they stretched and bent the branches of the gum trees. "If the branches break," they roared at Kirimumba, "we shall finally be on earth where we want to be!"

"But you will never get there alive!" Kirimumba warned them. "The trees in our Sky Land are big and strong, but not strong enough for you to forever be standing on the edges, bending the branches. Please! I love to live in these trees! Maybe the earth is beautiful *because* of our trees. Maybe the earth *needs* our trees to stay beautiful. Stop! Be careful!"

I hear you asking, "What does this have to do with bones?" Look! Look what I have in my hands. It is so heavy I can barely lift it. It is a bone. A *kadimakara* bone! Monsters have been in your dreams, and this is the bone of a real monster—a *kadimakara!* That frightens you, doesn't it? You think you will turn your head around and the monsters will be coming at you from behind right now! Ho, my children! You jumped in fright and surprise! Fear not. All that is left of them is their bones.

The earth had waters, flowers green,
And now the earth has bones.
The waters and the flowers green
Have turned to desert stones.

The earth, it used to be so flat,
And now it is so round.
The earth, it used to be so flat,
Until the bones came down.

The bones of kadimakara are here.
They're on our earth right now.
The bones of kadimakara are here,
And I will tell you how!

From *Day of the Moon Shadow: Tales with Ancient Answers to Scientific Questions.*
©1995. Libraries Unlimited. (800) 237-6124.

You see, my children, the *kadimakara* refused to listen to Kirimumba, and Kirimumba was right! Strong as the trees were, they could not withstand the weight of the great monsters bending them all day and all night. Branch after branch began to break off. Each branch had several monsters on it. Tumbling, tumbling, and tumbling through the land in the sky, one by one, each of them fell, crashing into the earth! Aeons and aeons of time passed. The gum nuts flew into the darkness of the Sky Land to become glistening stars. As the trees fell with the monsters on them, pieces of earth went flying all about and sent the earth spinning. Chunks of earth spun and flew, forming the great ball that is earth now, and the bones of the monsters crashing into the earth were buried deeper and deeper in the huge, round ball.

All of the leaves of the giant gum trees tumbled, and there was no longer any shade for the earth, at least not for our place here in the center of Australia. The land grew parched and bare. The lakes and rivers, so envied by the *kadimakara*, turned into salt-encrusted depressions in the hot, dry sand. The trunks of the gum trees slowly began to fall, too. When the trunks were no longer there in the Sky Land, three big holes were left instead.

The holes kept growing larger until they ran together, and the sky became one great, big, expansive hole. The Dieri tribe, our tribe, calls this hole *pura wilpanina!*

As for little Kirimumba, he fell to the earth, carried on a giant gum tree leaf that landed on a eucalyptus tree. As this happened, the spirit of the koala awoke from *dreamtime* in which all things of the universe begin. The koala spirit transformed Kirimumba into the first koala, that small, cute, and beautiful animal. Though Kirimumba could no longer sit on the gum trees he had so enjoyed in the Sky Land, he—and all koalas who came after him—spend their days and nights on the branches of the eucalyptus trees, eating their leaves forever!

So there, my children, is your answer about the sky! And there is your answer about the bones!

Other tribes say that the *kadimakara* grew, eating all the leaves and gum nuts on all of the three large trees until there were none left to eat. Then they starved and died. Yet, if this were so, their bones would now hang down from the branches, making a pathway to the sky for us to climb. Some say that the monsters may have grown dizzy watching the animals enjoying themselves on this earth and that they fainted, never to awaken again. There are many answers as to why they died, why they became extinct. Perhaps we shall never know for sure. Chant along with me, my children

Leader:	Response:
Bones!	Bones!
Bones!	Bones!
Kadimakara bones!	*Kadimakara* bones!
Monstrous bones!	Monstrous bones!
Bones from the Sky Land!	Bones from the Sky Land!
Bones!	Bones!
Bones!	Bones!
Kadimakara bones!	*Kadimakara* bones!
Oh, to think, they've all become extinct!	Oh, to think, they've all become extinct!
Bones!	Bones!
Bones!	Bones!
Kadimakara bones!	*Kadimakara* bones!
Extinct,	Extinct,
Extinct,	Extinct!
Kadimakara, extinct! (all together)	

References

Science

- Bakker, Robert T. 1986. *The Dinosaur Heresies*. New York: Zebra Books.

- Dixon, Dougal, et al. 1988. *The Macmillan Illustrated Encyclopedia of Dinosaurs and Prehistoric Animals: American Museum of Natural History*. New York: Macmillan.

- Morell, Virginia. 1987. "Announcing the Birth of a Heresy." *Discover Magazine* (March).

- Stout, William. 1981. *The Dinosaurs*. New York: Bantam Books.

- Wilford, John Noble. 1985. *The Riddle of the Dinosaur*. New York: Vintage Books.

Anthropology

- Scott, O. R. n.d. *Discover Australia: The Aborigines, Vol. 2*. Sydney, N.S.W.: Kenmure Press.

- Gunn, Aeneas. 1981. *We of the Never Never*. Richmond, Victoria, Australia: Hutchison.

- Isaacs, Jennifer. 1980. *Australian Dreaming: 40,000 Years of Aboriginal History*. Sydney; New York: Landsdowne Press.

- Chatwin, Bruce. 1987. *The Songlines*. New York: Penguin Books.

Folklore

- Berndt, Ronald Murray. 1980. *The Speaking Land: Myth and Story in Aboriginal Australia*. New York: Penguin Books.

- Mountford, Charles P., and Ainslie Roberts. 1980. *The First Sunrise*. Sydney; New York: Rigby.

- Reed, A. W. 1978. *Aboriginal Legends—Animal Tales*. Sydney: A. H. & A. W. Reed. ("Monsters of the Sky Land" was inspired by the traditional tale "Dinosaurs of the Sky" as found in this source.)

Music

- *Arnhem Land*. EMI, Australia. (Vol. 1).

- *Songs of Aboriginal Australia and Torres Strait*. Folkways 4102.

- *Songs of the Western Australia Desert Aborigines*. Folkways 4210.

What Is the Sky?

From "Monsters of the Sky Land"

Music and Lyrics by
JUDY GAIL

The sky is a big hole of no-thing, no earth and no wa-ter. The sky is a spi-rit of dark-ness and then one of light. The sky is an emp-ty piece of wood that ev'-ry-thing sits up-on. The sky was filled with monstrous crea-tures, but the mons-trous crea-tures are gone!

The instrumental parts in this song, occurring between the vocal parts, were intended for the Aboriginal didjeridoo, a reed instrument made of wood but having no holes for fingering. It drones like bagpipes and resonates like an oboe. A kazoo placed inside a hollow log or cardboard carpet roll will create the desired sound.

Chant of the Kadimakara

From "Monsters of the Sky Land"

Music and Lyrics by
JUDY GAIL

The students or audience repeats each phrase after the leader.

Tune the low E-string of the guitar down to D.

Song of the Earth

From "Monsters of the Sky Land"

Music and Lyrics by
JUDY GAIL

For this song, tune the low E-string of the guitar down to D.

From *Day of the Moon Shadow: Tales with Ancient Answers to Scientific Questions.* ©1995. Libraries Unlimited. (800) 237-6124. Copyright ©1987, ©1995, Poppykettle Enterprises, Inc., Miami, Florida. (305) 387-3683. International copyrights secured. All rights reserved.

Chant of the Bones

From "Monsters of the Sky Land"

Music and Lyrics by
JUDY GAIL

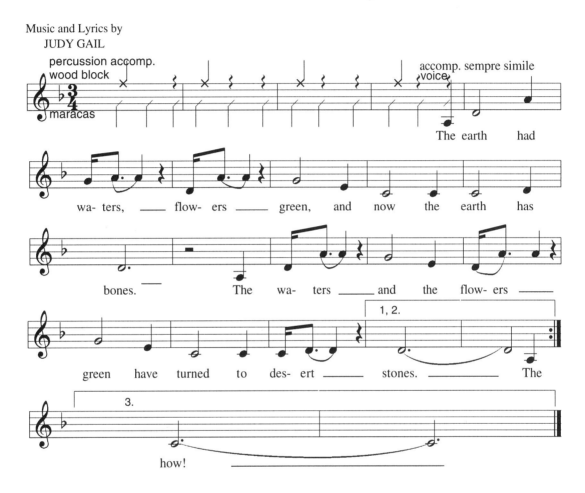

2. The earth, it used to be so flat,
   And now it is so round.
   The earth, it used to be so flat,
   Until the bones came down.

3. The bones of kadimakara are here.
   They're on our earth right now.
   The bones of kadimakara are here,
   And I will tell you how!

Kirimumba's Plea

From "Monsters of the Sky Land"

Music and Lyrics by
JUDY GAIL

You will break the bran- ches, lis- ten to me! —

ad lib didjeridoo

Put a- way your jeal- ous- y.

For- get the earth and its green- er- y.

I am Ki-ri mumba, lis- ten to me!

Song of Extinction

From "Monsters of the Sky Land"

Music and Lyrics by
JUDY GAIL

The students or audience repeats each phrase after the leader.

6
KIKU'S REFLECTION

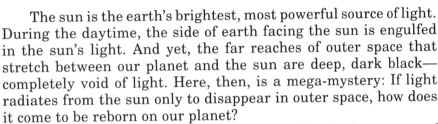

KIKU'S REFLECTION

A Story from Japan

How can we see our reflections when there is light?
How do fireflies flicker and glow in the night?
I wonder and ask, ask and wonder!

The sun is the earth's brightest, most powerful source of light. During the daytime, the side of earth facing the sun is engulfed in the sun's light. And yet, the far reaches of outer space that stretch between our planet and the sun are deep, dark black—completely void of light. Here, then, is a mega-mystery: If light radiates from the sun only to disappear in outer space, how does it come to be reborn on our planet?

The answer to this fascinating mystery lies in the process of reflection. Light is bundles of energy called photons. These photons travel in straight waves. We cannot see light unless these waves reflect or bounce off an object. Because there is nothing in outer space, not even air, to reflect light, it remains invisible. Once light hits earth, it is reflected back and forth on our planet, saturating our senses.

When light waves hit a completely smooth, shiny surface such as a mirror, they are reflected back in exactly the same condition with no distortion. This is why you can see a perfect reflection of yourself in a mirror. However, if light waves bounce off a rough object, the waves are diffused or spread out every which way in all directions. When you stand in front of a wall, the light bounces off you onto the wall. Instead of being reflected back in a perfect, undistorted image, the light waves bounce off in different directions. You can see the wall—but not your image in it.

All the different colors of the spectrum are created by light waves of different lengths. You can see part of this spectrum in a rainbow. The color of a light wave depends on its length. A long wavelength produces oranges and reds. Yellow is a medium wavelength. Short wavelengths are greens and blues. When all the wavelengths or colors are combined, they appear white, which is natural light. When light hits a rough object, such as an apple, all the colors of light are absorbed or drawn into the apple except the red wavelength. That is reflected back to our eyes. This is why the apple appears red. Likewise, the green leaves of the apple tree are absorbing all wavelengths of light except green.

There is another form of light created by a chemical process. The flashing lights of fireflies are produced by a chemical reaction called bioluminescence. Fireflies have five chemicals in their stomachs. When they breathe in oxygen, these chemicals are activated and combine to produce a glowing substance. This is what we see when we see the fireflies' light. Once again, the firefly breathes in oxygen. This time, however, a sixth chemical puts the light out. The female firefly waits in the grass and watches the male's light go on and off. She responds by turning her light on and off. Upon seeing this light, the male joins her in the grass to mate.

Thousands of years ago, people saw their reflections and had no idea how this was possible. Often, they did not even know that they were seeing a reflection of themselves and thought the reflection to be some other creature. Likewise, when they witnessed fireflies flickering on and off on a warm summer evening, they attributed magical powers to the insect, knowing nothing about chemical reactions and bioluminescence. The ancient Japanese culture had fascinating, nonscientific explanations for both reflections and the light of fireflies. The people of Japan called fireflies *hotaru* and believed these glowing insects to be the ghosts of dead human warriors returned to finish fighting their battles. Japanese families would go into the forest on summer evenings to watch fireflies just for fun. As they did so, they would tell stories of the *hotaru's* battles against evil.

The Japanese also had a ghostly explanation for reflections seen in mirrors. They believed that every day, as a person looked into their own mirror, little bits of the soul or spirit of that person were drawn out of the body and captured in the mirror. The reflection seen was really a ghost of the person who had looked into the mirror. It was also believed that, even after a person died, some of that person's spirit would remain captured in the mirror. If a living person looked into a mirror that had belonged to a dead person, the living person could see the dead person's face. The Japanese loved and honored mirrors because they believed that mirrors reflected the heart, or the feelings deep within each person. A person with loving and kind feelings would, therefore, look beautiful in the mirror's reflection. An evil or selfish person would see an ugly reflection. No one could fool the mirror!

The Japanese today have fascinating customs that are interesting to know about. For example, an individual person is representative of an entire family. If one family member does something good, the entire family is honored. Likewise, if one member of the family does something wrong or unacceptable, the entire family is shamed. It is important always to behave according to custom and to succeed in school and work to bring honor to the family.

When Japanese greet someone, they do not shake hands or hug or kiss. Instead, they bow to each other. The lower one bows, the more respect is shown. The Japanese eat with chopsticks, not forks, knives, and spoons. In Japan, people do not have a lot of furniture. They prefer an almost empty house, for they think that simplicity is elegant and beautiful. They line their floors with mats called *tatamis*. Instead of sitting on chairs or sofas, they kneel on their tatamis to eat, talk with their friends, and even to watch television.

Before entering a Japanese house, it is important to always take your shoes off, for you do not want to track dirt on the *tatamis*. You will not see bedrooms in a Japanese home, for economizing on space is important. The population of Japan is extremely large, and the islands that make up this country are small. Instead of bedrooms and beds, the Japanese have futons on which they sleep. They roll these up and store them away during the day, and at night, place them on the *tatamis* to sleep.

To the Japanese, leaving garbage on the streets in bags or containers for collection is unthinkable and unclean. Garbage collectors are respected and provided with spotless uniforms to wear. They come at specific times, and their trucks play music that signals their arrival. When people hear the music, they come outside with their garbage wrapped in containers that look almost like gift boxes tied with strings and lay these out for the friendly, smiling garbage collectors to pick up.

Japanese theater is filled with ornate costumes, beautiful shadow puppetry, and wonderful masks. Storytelling is appreciated, enjoyed, and respected. Often a storyteller uses masks while telling the tale. In this way, one storyteller can play several different characters simply by wearing a variety of masks while acting out the parts of all the characters in the story. Often, they use large fans as props. With imagination, these fans can represent anything: a sword, mirror, walking stick—even fireflies.

Imagine yourself traveling to hear a storyteller in Matsuyama, Japan, hundreds of years ago, when Japanese people held many magical and fanciful beliefs, such as those about mirrors and fireflies.

KIKU'S REFLECTION

A long time ago, there lived a man named Yosoji, his wife, Yoshiko, and their little daughter, Kiku. Although they were poor, they were a happy family who enjoyed each other's company more than anything else. One day, Yosoji, who was a merchant and traded goods, was called away to the distant city of Kyoto on business. Kiku was sad because she missed her kind father whenever he went away. To brighten her spirits, Yosoji promised, "If you are good and obedient to your mother while I am gone, I will bring you back a present from Kyoto. It will be something you have never seen the likes of before!"

Despite the exciting promise, Kiku watched with tears in her eyes as her father departed. Every day, Kiku would stand on a grassy hill outside the village, looking for Yosoji to return. One day, she saw his large grass hat bobbing as he walked. Joyfully, she ran and embraced him, singing

My father is home! Yosoji is home,
And I am so happy I'm singing a song!
Oh, look how he smiles, and I smile too.
Yosoji, my father, I really missed you.
He's brought me a gift, and I wonder if
It's what I've been dreaming and wishing it is!
My father is home! Yosoji is home,
And I am so happy I'm singing a song!

Yosoji removed his hat and sandals, entered the hut, and kneeled on the *tatami*. He removed a bamboo basket from his back and, watching the eager eyes of Kiku, reached inside. Slowly, he drew out a doll and placed it in his daughter's outstretched hands. Kiku had never seen a doll so beautiful. She carefully placed the perfect miniature lady on a shelf and stood gazing at it.

Yosoji then beckoned his wife to come stand at his side. Once again, he reached into the basket. This time, he pulled out a small object that he kept hidden in his hand. With loving eyes, he looked at his wife and said, "Dear Yoshi, my gift to you is also a beautiful lady, but she in no way compares with the doll given to our daughter. This one breathes and nourishes and loves. My gift to you is truly the most wondrous!" He presented Yoshiko with a metal mirror. On its back was a design of pine trees and storks. Yoshiko stared into

From *Day of the Moon Shadow: Tales with Ancient Answers to Scientific Questions.*
©1995. Libraries Unlimited. (800) 237-6124.

the mirror. At first, she thought another woman looked out at her, but Yosoji explained the mystery. "Mirrors are sacred," he said. "They reflect the same face a thousand times a thousand. They reflect the heart. May this mirror have the honor of reflecting your sweet face and heart for a long, long time."

Reflections of your life, my wife,
Shine with beauty gentle.
A picture of your soul within,
A soul with love so plentiful.

A woman with a spirit pure.
A heart of bird-like song.
A woman's love like comfort's wings,
You touch us all day long.

Look into the mirror, love.
Look, and you will see,
A wife and mother-person there,
My love, my dear Yoshi.

Not long after this joyous homecoming, Yoshiko grew very ill. She called Kiku to her side. Holding her young daughter's hand, she said, "Soon I will be joining our ancestors. My daughter, my little Kiku, I will never really leave you. Whenever you feel lonely, or whenever you need me, just look into my mirror, and I will be there!"

After saying these words, gentle Yoshiko died. In due time, Yosoji married again. His new wife, Miyuki, was a very good person and cared deeply for little Kiku, but she grew ever more jealous of the strong relationship between Yosoji and Kiku. She wished to be loved as though she were Kiku's blood mother. This jealousy blinded Miyuki's judgment and caused her to resent Kiku. She believed that Kiku did not like her.

One day, Miyuki saw Kiku sitting under a tree looking at a hidden object and murmuring to herself. Miyuki's vivid imagination made her think that Kiku was performing some evil magic—perhaps sticking pins into an image of her, trying to kill her! Miyuki grabbed a large stick and went after poor Kiku, chasing her out of the yard and out of the village yelling, "You evil child! Your behavior toward me has shamed your family. When I tell your father what you have done, he will never let you return to disgrace our home with your presence again!"

Kiku ran into the woods and stood trembling behind a tree, holding her mother's mirror. All she had been doing was looking at her dead mother's soul in the mirror. Her mother's face had appeared young and beautiful, not twisted in pain as it had on her death bed. Now Kiku pressed the mirror to her heart, which beat fast with fear. Totally bewildered, she wondered what thing she had done that was terrible enough to shame her family? She looked into the mirror. Her mother's usual smiling face was now filled with tears.

> *Mother, why do you cry?*
> *Such big tears within your eyes.*
> *Are you sad that Miyuki scolds me?*
> *Mother, I wish you could hold me.*
> *Mother, why do you cry?*
> *Mother, why did you die?*

Night soon fell, filling the woods with its darkness. Frightened, Kiku found solace in the warm summer air and soft, deep grass where she lay as sleep overtook her. When the sun arose, she awakened with a hollow feeling in her stomach. Placing the mirror in her pocket, she left in search of food. She found some blackberries and had no sooner begun to eat when she heard a noise behind her. With a thumping heart, she quickly turned around to see a young boy. He had a kind, compassionate face as he spoke, "You look so frightened and hungry. Are you lost?"

"Yes, I am. I have nowhere to go, for I have been told I can never return home again."

"Come with me to my house. You can be my sister, for I have no sisters or brothers. I'll take care of you."

The young boy held out his hand, and Kiku took it, feeling fortunate to have made such a kind friend, but as she walked beside him, doubt began to form in her mind. Something felt wrong. His hand! Her father had told her about a strange goblin called the Jikkinninnkki that could magically change its appearance to look like anyone or thing it wanted. The Jikkinninnkki could easily lure innocent victims into its lair, then change back into its goblin shape and enslave its captives forever! Because it was already dead, though seemingly alive, its hands were always icy cold—just like the young boy's hand that she now held! "What will I do?" Kiku thought. Lost in thought, Kiku failed to look where she was walking and tripped over a tree root. As she fell, her mother's mirror slipped from her pocket and lay glimmering in the sun.

"What is that?" the boy asked.

"It is the mirror of my dead mother. I keep it with me so I can look into her beautiful face whenever I want."

"Let me look into it. I like pretty things!" To himself, the boy chanted

I am a Jikkinninnkki
Jikkinninnkki, Jikki Jikki Nninnkki Nninnkki.
I am a Jikkinninnkki
I like pretty things!

Kiku doesn't know what I am.
I can look like what I want.
I can look just like a man, oh,
Jikki Jikki Nninnkki Nninnkki—HA! Jikkinninnkki!

Now I appear a handsome boy,
A pretty girl's joy,
With her pretty mirror toy.
I like pretty things!

I'll get precious little Kiku
And her precious mirror,
Lure her toward the river,
And there she will sink in!

She'll become like a pet
To our Jikkinninnkki set,
Like a furry little dog,
Or a cat, a bird, a frog,

For I am a Jikkinninnkki,
Jikkinninnkki Jikki Jikki Nninnkki Nninnkki!
I am a Jikkinninnkki!
I like pretty things!

The boy picked up the mirror and looked straight into its surface. He did not see Kiku's mother, nor did he see a handsome young boy. Mirrors reflect the heart. Mirrors cannot be fooled! The Jikkinninnkki saw a horrible, grotesque goblin. In dreadful fright, he screamed, and his screams echoed throughout the woods. Dropping to all fours, he quickly burrowed down into a deep hole in the ground, disappearing from sight!

Kiku picked up the mirror and looked into it, wondering what her mother had done to scare the boy so. Still frightened, Kiku ran. Her shoe fell off, and she cut her foot on sharp rocks. Bramble branches and their thorns tore at her hair and body. Exhausted, she fell into a clump of clover and fell asleep. She awoke to darkness and began to cry as she realized how lost she was. Looking into the mirror, she pleaded, "Please, mother, help me before the Jikkinninnkki finds me again. I don't know what Miyuki told my father about me, but in my heart, I know he still loves me. Guide me back to him, and I will do my best to make peace with Miyuki, so the three of us may live in harmony together."

Through her tears, Kiku became aware of a golden glow. She rubbed her eyes and stared in amazement. Rising from the clover were thousands of fireflies. To Kiku, these were none other than the *hotaru* warriors, with their golden tails lighting the forest. They flew around and around Kiku as their song buzzed, echoing through the forest.

From *Day of the Moon Shadow: Tales with Ancient Answers to Scientific Questions.*
©1995. Libraries Unlimited. (800) 237-6124.

We are flutt'ring, flitting fireflies,
Bioluminescence lighting up the skies,
While in the forest, frightened Kiku cries.
We must save Kiku from the Jikkinninnkki!

Light the way, for I see her father comes.
Light the way! In his fear, see how he runs.
Together we shed bright light like the sun.
We must save Kiku from the Jikkinninnkki!

Fireflies, fireflies, light up your lights!
Don't light them dimly, light them very bright!
Together we create an illuminating sight.
We must save Kiku from the Jikkinninnkki!
We must save Kiku from the Jikkinninnkki!

A few fireflies broke away, then the others followed. Not wanting to lose them, Kiku followed the *hotaru* through the woods. They flew faster and faster, and Kiku, exhausted, struggled to keep up with them. Thinking she could run no more, renewed energy soared through her as she heard a familiar voice calling her name. She ran toward the sound as the fireflies led her in its direction. It was her father's voice, ringing with love and desperation throughout the woods.

"Here I am, Father! Here! Here!" Before Kiku could yell again, her father had lifted her up in his arms as the fireflies danced around them, then disappeared deep into the forest again.

"Oh, my daughter, my daughter. How happy I am to find you well. I feared for your life when I heard the scream of the Jikkinninnkki!"

"Father, please do not be angry with me. I do not know what I did to disgrace our family so!"

Kiku looked over her father's shoulder and saw Miyuki walking toward her. Miyuki spoke, "Your father explained to me that you were only looking into your mother's mirror. You were not wishing me any evil. I am so ashamed of myself for being ignorant and foolish."

Kiku, please forgive what I've done.
I was jealous, mean, and cruel.
Just because I'm not the one
Who really is your mother!

Kiku, please forgive what I've done.
I will love you in my way.
Kiku, please let me be the one
Whom you can call your friend.

Kiku looked into the mirror again. Her mother was smiling. She put the mirror in her pocket, took her father's hand on one side and Miyuki's hand on the other, and the three of them walked home together. Yosoji sang with utter joy

My child is home! Yes, Kiku is home,
And I am so happy, I'm singing this song!
Oh, look how she smiles, and I smile too.
Oh, Kiku, my child, I really missed you.
You've brought me a gift, the very best gift,
The gift is my child, my Kiku it is!
My child is home! Yes, Kiku is home,
And I am so happy I'm singing this song!

References

Science

- Cobb, Vick. *Light Action!* 1993. *Amazing Experiments with Optics*. New York: HarperCollins.

- Harre, Rom. 1981. *Great Scientific Experiments*. Oxford: Phaidon Press.

- Hoban, Tana. 1990. *Shadows and Reflections*. Greenwillow Books.

- Newman, Jay Hartley, and Lee Scott Newman. *The Mirror Book: Using Reflective Surfaces in Art, Craft and Design*. New York: Crown, 1978.

- *Sight, Light and Color*. 1984. (Science Universe Series). New York: Arco Publishing.

Anthropology

- Ayrton, Matilda Chaplin. 1879. *Child-Life in Japan & Japanese Child-Stories*. London: Griffith.

- Baines, John D. 1994. *Japan: Country Fact File Series*. Austin, TX: Raintree Steck-Vaughn.

- Colcutt, Martin; Marius Jansen; and Isao Kumakura. 1988. *Cultural Atlas of Japan*. New York: Facts on File.

- Hartshorne, Anna C. 1902. *Japan and Her People*. Philadelphia: H. T. Coates.

- Joya, Mock. n.d. *Quaint Customs and Manners of Japan*. Tokyo: The Tokyo News Service LTD.

- Lebra, Takie Sugiyama. 1976. *Japanese Patterns of Behavior*. Honolulu: University of Hawaii Press.

- Sawyers, Martha, and William Reusswig. 1961. *Far East*. New York: Grosset and Dunlap.

Folklore

- Inoue, Yasunari. 1954. *The Izu Dancer*. Rutland, VT: Charles E. Tuttle.

- James, Grace. 1987. *Green Willow and Other Japanese Fairy Tales*. New York: Crown.

- *Myths and Legends of Japan*. 1913. London: George G. Harrap. ("Kiku's Reflection" was inspired by the traditional tale "The Mirror of Matsuyama" as found in this source.)

- Tyler, Royall, ed. and trans. 1987. *Japanese Tales*. New York: Pantheon Fairy Tale and Folklore Library.

Music

- Lee, Riley Kelly. *Shakuhachi Honkyoku: Japanese Flute Music*. Folkways 4229.

- Stern, Isaac. *Classical Melodies of Japan*. RCA.

- *Traditional Folksongs of Japan*. Folkways 4534 AB, 4534 CD.

My Father Is Home/My Child Is Home

From "Kiku's Reflection"

Music and Lyrics by
JUDY GAIL

The second verse is sung at the end of the story.

From *Day of the Moon Shadow: Tales with Ancient Answers to Scientific Questions.* ©1995. Libraries Unlimited. (800) 237-6124. Copyright ©1987, ©1995, Poppykettle Enterprises, Inc., Miami, Florida. (305) 387-3683. International copyrights secured. All rights reserved.

Song of the Mirror

From "Kiku's Reflection"

Music and Lyrics by
JUDY GAIL

In keeping with the ethnic flavor of this song, it is best to play fifths with the left hand.

Kiku's Lament

From "Kiku's Reflection"

Music and Lyrics by
JUDY GAIL

This song should be sung plaintively. It is best accompanied by
a rolling chord with the notes played individually in two-four time.

Song of the Jikkinninnkki

From "Kiku's Reflection"
Page 1

Music and Lyrics by
JUDY GAIL

Song of the Jikkinninnkki

From "Kiku's Reflection"
Page 2

Song of the Fireflies

From "Kiku's Reflection"
Page 1

Music and Lyrics by
JUDY GAIL

With an electronic keyboard, this song sounds good using a plectra or mandolin accompaniment. The left hand is best played in octaves rather than chords.

Song of the Fireflies

From "Kiku's Reflection"

Page 2

The Stepmother's Plea

From "Kiku's Reflection"

Music and Lyrics by
JUDY GAIL

Ki-ku, please for-give what I've done. I was jeal-ous, mean, and cruel.

Just be-cause I'm not the — one who real-ly is your mo- ther!

Ki-ku, please for-give what I've done. I will love you in my way.

Ki-ku, please let me be the one whom you can call your friend.

Accompanied on guitar or keyboard, this song sounds best with a broken chord played repeating the rhythm of 1 and 2 and 3 and 4 and 1 and 2 and 3 and 4 and so on.

7
They Called Him Brother

THEY CALLED HIM BROTHER

A Story from the Naskapi Indians of North America

Is it true that together wolves howl and play?
Why are there so few wolves left today?
I wonder and ask, ask and wonder!

As technology and ever-growing cities remove people farther and farther from nature, people study nature using modern scientific techniques. Native Americans understood much about animals like the wolf simply from observing and living with them. Today, scientists study wolves using radio transmitters to trace tagged wolves and high-tech cameras to photograph wolves from helicopters. Wildlife managers even move wolves back to areas where they used to live before huge numbers of them were slaughtered for their fur and for livestock protection.

Europeans who immigrated to this country brought with them tales of werewolves, stories like "Little Red Riding Hood," and the belief that the wolf was a vicious animal that killed for the sake of killing. Native Americans knew this was not so. Today, scientists teach what Native Americans already knew, that wolves are highly intelligent, social animals who, as carnivores, or meat eaters, must hunt for their food. Unlike some people, wolves kill only in order to eat!

Wolves, which are on the endangered species list, live in packs of 8 to 10. The leader is called the alpha male, and his mate, the alpha female, is most often the only female in the pack to bear pups.

Wolves mate for life. The pack includes leaders, assistants, subordinates, and even scapegoats—wolves who are teased and pushed aside and always get the least nutritious remains of a kill. These scapegoats often become lone wolves and leave the pack. If two wolves fight for leadership or for a mate, or if a lone wolf is attacked for trespassing on a pack's territory, the combatants do not kill each other.

Instead, the wolf who realizes that he is the loser lies down and exposes the part of his neck where the jugular vein lies. The winner makes the gesture of biting the loser's neck but does not

121

actually do so. In this way, the fight is declared over, with the loser admitting defeat.

All members of the pack care for the young and discipline them with paw slaps and a variety of sounds. Older brothers and sisters play with younger pups, and many of their games imitate hunting and the rituals of accepting one's place in the pack. Playing for wolves is both fun and a learning experience.

Wolves are highly communicative animals, and they know the howls of their own pack. When a lone wolf howls, a pack answers with a mixture of howls, growls, and barks, warning the strange wolf to stay away. Baby wolves make loud yelping and squealing sounds. These keep potential predators away from the den while the parents are out hunting for food. Wolves howl up to 12 different harmonics. When the pack howls together, often to celebrate a good kill and full stomachs, they actually harmonize like a chorus! They also communicate by smiling, grimacing, frowning, snarling, and making other facial gestures.

The wolf pack hunts together, and each wolf has a vital role in the hunt. The pack stalks its prey, often large animals such as caribou and moose. They run together steadily for hours until the hunted animal begins to tire. Then they zero in on their prey. One wolf runs in front of the animal and distracts it, while the other pack members surprise it by attacking from the back and sides, trying to break one of its legs so that the animal can no longer run. Wolves do not kill healthy members of a herd. They attack older or weaker animals or young animals that have gone astray during the chase. Hunting is difficult, and when the prey is finally killed, the wolves down 20 to 30 pounds of meat, hide, sinew, bones, and hair in one meal, not knowing when they might be successful at another hunt. The saying "wolfing it down" originally described the way wolves gobble down their food!

When Native Americans were the only inhabitants of North America, they respected and identified with the wolf. They even learned how to hunt caribou, moose, and bear from observing wolves hunting. Like the wolf, they also killed only for survival. They had to learn to use every part of the animals they killed: skins for clothing and shelter; organs such as the bladder for carrying; bones for tools; hair for warmth; and feces for fuel. Like the wolf, they hunted in groups. From the top of a hill they would spot their prey, say a herd of caribou. They would run at a distance, yet from a vantage point where they could follow the path of the herd. Like wolves, they would run at a brisk pace for many miles. Then one man would crouch, whistling low to the others. Without another word, the men would run in different directions, and, like each wolf, each man knew what his role would be in attacking the prey animal.

The Naskapi Indians were seminomadic, meaning they had permanent dwellings that they left at certain times of the year to follow animal herds. The Naskapi lived in northeastern Canada, in a bleak land with almost no vegetation and bitterly cold winters. For centuries they hunted the same caribou herds as the wolves. Hunting was a tremendous responsibility, for if the hunters were not successful, starvation, weakness, sickness, and death could come to the entire tribe. For a Naskapi hunter, failure to kill in a hunt showed the hunter's ignorance of how he should behave toward animals. And, far worse, it showed his lack of respect for the animals. This was considered evil, for it could bring many misfortunes from the spirits to the hunter and the tribe!

The Naskapi believed there was good meat and bad meat. Good meat was like medicine and came from herbivores, animals who eat plants. This hunting tribe understood the plant world to be a pharmacopoeia, a world from which people acquired cures for ailments and illnesses. Eating an animal that ate the plants from this pharmacopoeia would impart great health and strength. Animals like the wolf, which ate only meat, were not hunted and eaten because they would not provide the necessary health and strength. Cows would not be considered good meat, even though they are herbivores, because they are domesticated. They are tamed, no longer able to defend themselves and dependent on humans for their survival. A domesticated animal has no Animal Master, therefore, it has no spirit!

The Naskapi called the meat of animals such as the wild caribou "sacred meat." When a sacred animal was killed, they believed its spirit went to a spirit place: the Caribou House, where the Animal Master lived. The mountains in Caribou House were white, not from snow and ice but from caribou hair that had fallen on the ground over centuries and centuries as caribou ran there, shedding their white hair. The piles of shed hair were almost the height of a man and were filled with cast-off caribou antlers.

The spirits of the dead caribou and the new caribou bodies that would bear these spirits lived at Caribou House with the Animal Master. Surrounding Caribou House were other animals that were fiercer and larger than their counterparts sent out into the world. The Naskapi feared these legendary animals. In the harsh climate where they lived, the Naskapi could not always find animals to hunt. During these times of famine, when food was scarce or not available, a tribe had to conduct a ceremony offering gifts to the Animal Master, or someone had to go into the awesome land of Caribou House and directly face the Animal Master, convincing him to release game for the tribe to eat.

According to Naskapi legend, the Animal Master, out of whose head gigantic, gold antlers protruded, would admonish the humble visitor never to forget that the spirit of the animal is sacred and must be respected. He would remind the visitor to learn from the wolf, who understood his teaching well, that killing must be done only when necessary. He would warn that the slain animal must never be eaten without proper ceremony. This ceremony was called *mokoshan*.

Imagine yourself to be a Naskapi Indian centuries ago. A sacred animal has been hunted and killed. *Mokoshan* has been observed, and now, lest the tribe forget where food comes from and the importance of respecting the spirits of the animals, the tribal storyteller tells her tale.

THEY CALLED HIM BROTHER

It was the beginning of time for us. There were no other animals then, only us people. The spirits had come to the shaman and given a vision that a cold season was coming, a very cold season. Cold white powder would cover the earth like a thick blanket. We would not be able to find our food—rhubarb and licorice plants, wild onions and birch and willow leaves.

It was then that a warrior called Swift-as-the-Wind said, "I was not named Swift-as-the-Wind for no reason. There is no time to waste! I will go and seek food that will give us more strength, food that will not be buried under the snows of the season of whiteness and death. I will take my brother Strong-as-the-River with me. We will travel to the Land of Spirits to ask for food to live!"

A Naskapi must be brave to survive. Swift-as-the-Wind and Strong-as-the-River were brave. Around the fire that night, our tribe beat the drums and chanted, calling on the spirits to make the brothers' journey safe and fruitful.

Spirits, hear us and give.
Give us food so we may live!
Spirits, hear our desp'rate cry!
To eat when snows fall from the sky!
Spirits, hear us! Spirits, hear us! Spirits, HEAR US!

The brothers left. For three days they paddled their birchbark canoe through the waters, following the beat of their hearts, which told them where the Land of the Spirits lay. They camped on shore. On the fourth morning, when they awoke, they saw a large mountain range before them. They set off on foot toward it. The path was difficult, filled with rocks and crevices and steep hills to climb. The winds blew, but the two brothers pressed onward. They saw nothing but white mountains before them and said, "This must be the cold white powder in the vision of the shaman."

Finally, they reached the great mountain and began to climb. They touched the whiteness all about them, but it was not cold. In fact, it warmed them after their trek through the icy wind. They picked up some of the whiteness and held it between their fingertips. They smelled it and rubbed it on their faces. Never before had they seen or felt or smelled anything like it, for what they held in their hands was the hair of the caribou, and in the

From *Day of the Moon Shadow: Tales with Ancient Answers to Scientific Questions.*
©1995. Libraries Unlimited. (800) 237-6124.

beginning of time for us, we did not know what a caribou was. They would later learn that they had reached the sacred land of Caribou House.

All about them were strange and beautifully shaped creatures covered with coats of different colors. At moments, the brothers clung together in utter dread, for some of these colorful creatures were larger than anything they had ever seen, even when dreaming. The creatures did not threaten them or even come near them. Soon the brothers lost their fear and allowed their curiosity to turn into joy. "Look," Swift-as-the-Wind cried, "There is a little stranger hopping on two twig-like legs, and, as it spreads its strange arms, it soars into the air!"

Before Strong-as-the-River could reply, his eyes set upon a wondrous sight. "Brother, here is another stranger—this one has four legs. Look at its head—it must be a head, for it has eyes and a mouth! And its head has small tree branches growing out of it!" The brothers did not know about antlers yet.

"We must be in the Land of the Spirits!" Swift-as-the-Wind cried, glad that they had followed the beat of their hearts to find their way there.

This must be the Land of the Spirits,
For stranger things we've never seen:
Some with four legs, some with two,
Who in the air are swift as can be!

Some with short hair, some with long hair,
Some with spears above their eyes!
Some with long ears, some with short ears,
Some on land, and some in the skies!

Listen to the sounds they make!
Bellow! Snort! Chirp! Neigh! Howl!
This must be the Land of the Spirits!

At this very moment, the most wondrous creature of all appeared before them. His presence overwhelmed the brothers, as the sun shone on solid gold antlers that glittered over his magnificent, golden brown face and body. First he bellowed, and the brothers' bodies shook to the vibrations echoing from mountain peak to mountain peak. Then he spoke in the Algonquian tongue of the two young warriors:

"I am Animal Master, chief and ruler of all the creatures you see here, for they are called "animals"! They will not harm you, for you have never harmed them. What is it you wish of me?"

"Animal Master," Swift-as-the-Wind answered, awestruck and trying to make his voice heard, though it wanted to stay stuck in his throat, "a vision has come to our shaman, a vision of a season of cold that shall soon be upon us. White powder will cover the plants that are our only food. We will be hungry. Can you help us?"

Animal Master looked the two young men over. He searched their eyes for signs of the honesty and integrity of their inner souls. After all, animals were sacred, and he could not risk betraying those whom he ruled. What he saw reassured him, and he spoke once more. "Yes, I can help. I will send many animals to your dwelling place. You will have to hunt for them—and kill them in order to eat them! Have you any questions?"

Strong-as-the-River, with great respect in his voice, asked, "What is "hunt," and what is "kill"?"

"You shall come to know. But before I send the animals to your dwelling, you must make a promise to me. Tell your tribe of it, and make them vow to keep the promise, too! You must keep this promise forever—or your food will disappear! I command that, as hunters, you promise to respect animals! You must never kill them, except when hungry. You must never waste any of their flesh, their bones, their hide, hair, or fur. Their spirits must never be insulted or ridiculed. And when you kill an animal and then eat its body for your sustenance, you must always first hold a ceremony called *mokoshan,* in which you give thanks to the spirit of the animal. As long as you and all the hunters of your tribe keep this promise, I will continue to send the animal spirits of the dead animals to you in new animal bodies."

The moment he finished speaking, Animal Master ran toward Strong-as-the-River. Terrified, Strong-as-the-River ran, trying to outrun Animal Master, but this great spirit hunter stalked and cornered him, no matter what jutting rock or mound of whiteness he tried to hide behind. Finally, Strong-as-the-River's strength gave out. He dropped to the ground, and the powerful Animal Master pierced him with his gold antlers and killed him!

Swift-as-the-Wind leaped to his brother's side and cried, "He is dead! My brother is dead! How could you do this to him?"

From *Day of the Moon Shadow: Tales with Ancient Answers to Scientific Questions.*
©1995. Libraries Unlimited. (800) 237-6124.

"How can you kill an animal?" Animal Master replied. "For that is what killing is! I have hunted and killed your brother. There is no difference between your brother and the animals you will kill!"

Swift-as-the-Wind immediately understood the message, that all life is equally sacred! Knowing that his message was understood, Animal Master breathed life back into Strong-as-the-River, who, much to the joy of his brother, stood up alive once again!

Animal Master then turned to Swift-as-the-Wind and said, "I shall give great powers to you. When you return to your tribe, you shall become a great healer and will be known as Swift-as-the-Wolf, for the wolf is an animal of high spirit, deep loyalty, and sharp mind! Before your first hunt, you must take your hunters to watch the wolf, for this animal will teach you how to hunt and survive. Go now and remember this":

> *Hunting is sacred, for all creatures have a spirit.*
> *Never forget the promise made to me.*
> *A world without animals is a barren lonely world,*
> *And one where all creatures will die hungry!*

The brothers returned to the tribe with their good news. Soon, animals ran all about the land, making it more beautiful and richer than ever before. The tribes did as Animal Master commanded. First, they watched the wolf to learn what to do. As the wolves chose a leader of the pack, they chose a hunter chief. As the wolves hunted together, the hunters hunted together. As the wolves knew how to follow the tracks and scents of animals, the hunters learned to do this, too.

And then it happened that on one hunt, a huge, growling bear ran after them. They had never seen a bear before and had yet to learn the dangerous work of hunting this animal. Strong-as-the-River, now Hunting Chief, ran in front of the charging creature and lunged at its throat with his spear. The arrows of the other hunters flew at the powerful animal but seemed only to prick its outer hide. The bear leaped forward, and its claws pierced the air—and then the chest of Strong-as-the-River. The hunter fell in a puddle of his own blood.

From *Day of the Moon Shadow: Tales with Ancient Answers to Scientific Questions.*
©1995. Libraries Unlimited. (800) 237-6124.

Just then, silently, from behind the trees, a pack of wolves appeared. The leader of the pack jumped toward the bear, while the other wolves snarled and barked, biting the bear on all sides. The confused animal did not know which way to turn. While the bear's eyes looked away from Strong-as-the-River, a hunter lifted the wounded man and carried him back to the camp.

The wolves continued their attack on the bear, each one playing its important role in the kill. The hunters now stood silently behind the trees, watching and learning from the wolves how to hunt this amazing animal. At last, the leader of the pack, jaws gaping, leaped at the bear and bit its throat, delivering the final death blow. The hunters spoke with their eyes to the tired wolves, thanking them for their knowledge and courage. They returned to their camp.

Swift-as-the-Wolf, now the tribe's honored healer, knew he must act quickly to save the life of his brother. He carried Strong-as-the-River to the river. Then he placed a wolf skin on his own head and back, a wolf skin granted to him when the leader of a wolf pack, which the hunters had befriended, had died of old age. The head of the wolf covered his head.

He painted the wolf's face and paws red, the color of the spirit of life. The drums began to beat as the men and women of the tribe chanted

Ai ai ai ai ai ai ai ai ai ai ai!
Ai ai ai ai ai ai ai ai ai ai ai!
Ai ai ai ai ai ai ai ai ai ai ai!
Ai ai ai ai ai ai ai ai AI!

Swift-as-the-Wolf danced around his dying brother with the movements of a wolf. He howled four times, "Ahooo, ahooo, ahooo, ahooo!" He continued to howl while lifting the wolf skin up and down over his head. As he did this, Strong-as-the-River began to lift his head up and down. Swift-as-the-Wolf moved toward the river, howling the howl of a mother wolf calling her pups to follow her.

Strong-as-the-River stood up, and, like a wolf pup obeying its mother's calls, followed his brother to the river and then into it.

The drumbeat changed, and the chanting grew louder as the tribe howled in harmony like a chorus of wolves, "Ahooo, ahooo, ahooo, ahooo, ahooo, ahooo!" They stopped. Now all that could be heard was Swift-as-the-Wolf howling the cry of the lone wolf. Pierced by this cry, Strong-as-the-River stood up like a loyal member of the pack, ready to fend off the stranger. He stretched his wounded body to its full height and howled, "Ahoooooooooo!" As he did so, blood gushed from his wound. Swift-as-the-Wolf then gestured the licking movement of a wolf healing its wounds with its tongue. He pulled his brother under the cold river water, then lifted him out. Again, he howled the mother wolf's beckoning call to her pups and walked out of the river. Strong-as-the-River followed. The blood from his wound flowed no more. He was healed!

The two brothers went inside to smoke the pipe of peace and eat the strengthening meat of the bear. Many prayers were said by the hunters while the meat was cut in a ceremonial room made for *mokoshan*. The women of the tribe chanted and prayed as they prepared the hide and other parts of the animal for their many uses. The grateful hunters had left much of the meat for the wolves, who had bravely shown the hunters how to hunt bear.

Strong-as-the-River spoke before eating the sacred meat, "It is you, Great Bear, that gives us our life! And it is you, my brother, who saved my life!"

"No, my brother," Swift-as-the-Wolf answered. "It is Brother Wolf who taught me what I know. It is Brother Wolf who saved your life!"

From *Day of the Moon Shadow: Tales with Ancient Answers to Scientific Questions.*
©1995. Libraries Unlimited. (800) 237-6124.

Brother Wolf, you taught us how to hunt!
Brother Wolf, you taught us how to cure!
Brother Wolf, you taught us how to share!
Brother Wolf, you taught us how to care!

Wolf, we call you Brother!
Wolf, we call you Brother!
Wolf, we call you Brother!
Wolf, we call you Brother!
Wolf, we call you Brother!
Wolf, we call you Brother!
Ahoooo! Ahooo! Ahooo! Ahooo!

References

Science

- Barrett, Norman S. 1991. *Wolves and Wild Dogs*. New York: Franklin Watts.

- Fox, Michael W. 1992. *The Soul of the Wolf*. New York: Lyons & Burford.

- Lawrence, R. D. 1986. *In Praise of Wolves*. New York: Henry Holt.

- Lopez, Barry Holstun. 1978. *Of Wolves and Men*. New York: Scribner's.

- Mech, L. David. 1991. *The Way of the Wolf*. Stillwater, MN: Voyageur Press.

- ———. 1977. "Where Can the Wolf Survive?" *National Geographic* 152, no. 4 (October): 519-37.

- Scott, Barry. 1979. *The Kingdom of Wolves*. New York: Putnam.

- *Wolf Facts*. 1987. Washington, DC: Defenders of Wildlife.

- *Wolves and Humans: Volunteer Training Packet*. 1983. 3 vols. The Science Museum of Minnesota.

Anthropology

- Campbell, Joseph. 1988. *The Power of Myth*. New York: Doubleday.

- Lopez, Barry Holstun. 1978. *Of Wolves and Men*. New York: Scribner's.

- Richardson, Boyce. 1991. *Strangers Devour the Land*. Post Mills, VT: Chelsea Green.

- *Wolves and Humans: Volunteer Training Packet*. 1983. 3 vols. The Science Museum of Minnesota.

Folklore

- Erdoes, Richard, and Alfonso Ortiz. 1984. *American Indian Myths and Legends*. New York: Pantheon Books.

- Lopez, Barry Holstun. 1978. *Of Wolves and Men*. New York: Scribner's.

- Norman, Howard, ed. 1990. *Northern Tales: Traditional Stories of Eskimo and Indian Peoples*. New York: Pantheon Books.

- *Wolves and Humans: Volunteer Training Packet*. 1983. 3 vols. The Science Museum of Minnesota.

Music

- *An Anthology of North American Indian and Eskimo Music*. Folkways FE 4541.

- *Music and Legend of the Naskapi*. Folkways 4253 & 4541.

Chant to the Spirits

From "They Called Him Brother"

Music and Lyrics by
JUDY GAIL

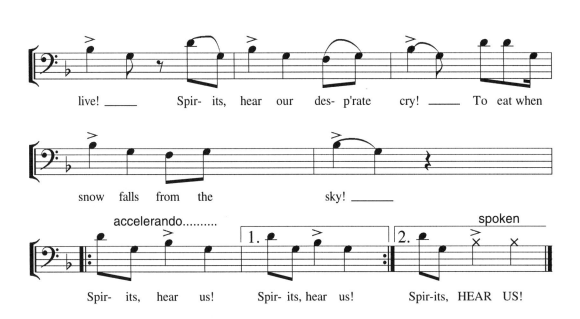

Land of the Spirits

From "They Called Him Brother"

Music and Lyrics by
JUDY GAIL

Hunting Is Sacred

From "They Called Him Brother"

Music and Lyrics by
JUDY GAIL

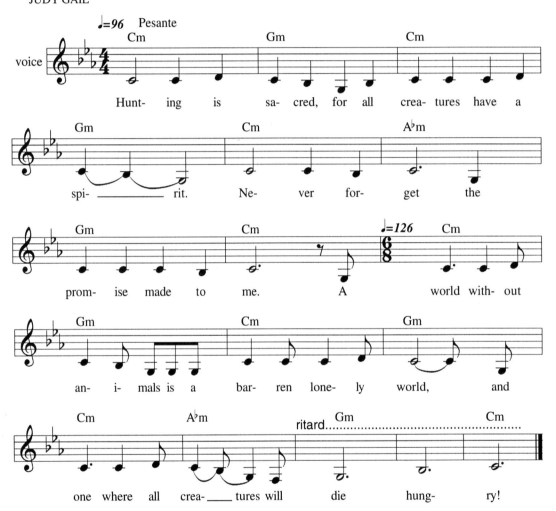

This song may be accompanied solely with rattles or also with a keyboard.

Chant of the Tribe

From "They Called Him Brother"

Music and Lyrics by
JUDY GAIL

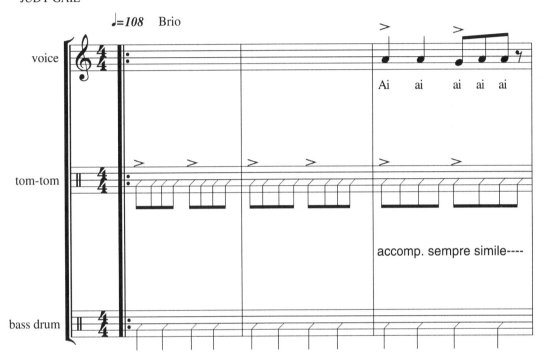

Brother Wolf

From "They Called Him Brother"

Music and Lyrics by
JUDY GAIL

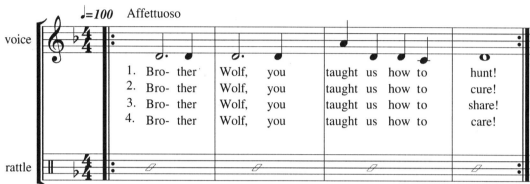

Repeat this section 4x to repeat sing all 4 verses.
Continue the rattle in a 1 2 3 4 beat and add the tom-tom and bass drum.

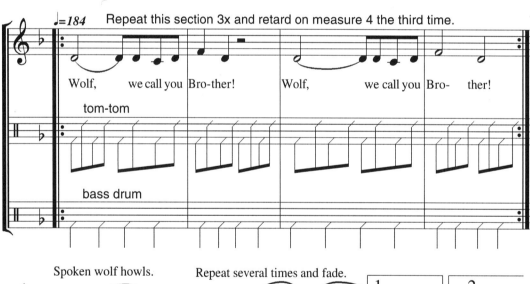

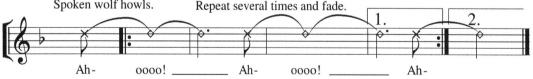

8
SPIRITS OF THE DANCING DEAD

SPIRITS OF THE DANCING DEAD

A Story from the Inuit of the Central Arctic

How do magnetic fields and electricity
Create the wondrous northern lights for us to see?
I wonder and ask, ask and wonder!

On certain nights, primarily in spring and autumn, an awesome sight lights up the arctic skies. The aurora borealis shimmers and glistens like a giant curtain of red, green, gold, purple, and blue. This phenomenon, also called the northern lights, is caused by atomic particles—protons and electrons that stream from the sun.

The sun is a gaseous mass and is constantly active. It creates eruptions, explosions, bubbles, flashes, and flares that result in solar wind. The surface of the sun sends tiny particles called atoms outward in all directions. Each of these atoms has a nucleus, and, traveling around the nucleus, much as the planets revolve around the sun, are tiny, charged particles called electrons. These electrons travel at a speed of about 300 miles per second. The stream of these electrical particles is what we call the solar wind. This wind travels far out into space, past the planets. When the particles that make up this wind reach the earth, they strike the upper atmosphere, particularly near the north and south magnetic poles.

The earth is surrounded by a magnetosphere, an electrically and magnetically charged area. This magnetosphere acts as a shield to keep solar particles and solar wind away from the earth. However, at the North and South Poles, it draws them in. The electric particles that make up the solar wind bombard the earth's magnetosphere, creating further electrical energy as the electrons move back and forth from their paths around the nuclei of the atoms of which they are part.

The earth's atmosphere is made up of many gases. As electrons flow through these gases, they excite them and cause them to glow. Different gases, when electrically excited, glow in different colors: Nitrogen glows purple; oxygen, blue; others are gold, green, or red. These gases, excited by the solar wind, create a magnificent sight of spiraling, streaking colors throughout the night sky. In the region of the North Pole, this phenomenon is called the aurora borealis. At the South Pole, it is called the aurora australis. The Inuit, or Eskimos of the Central Arctic, call it the *arsharshar.*

The aurora borealis is a common sight over Canada and Alaska. Occasionally, the sun's activity creates solar winds of such magnitude that the particles break through the earth's electromagnetic shield over other areas far to the south. But this is rare. The variable solar wind sometimes causes currents to flow in the earth itself. These earth currents affect the flow of electricity to electronics connected to underground conductors. When the Alaska pipeline was constructed directly across the auroral zone, the builders had to spend a great deal of time studying this problem in order to prevent earth currents, caused by the aurora borealis, from affecting the pipeline's operations.

Today, we know the scientific facts that explain the cause of the northern lights. Before the advent of telescopes, space probes, and other instruments that help give us answers to phenomena like the aurora borealis, people saw the magnificent lights in the sky but had no idea what caused them. The Inuit sensed the great powers of these lights and how they might affect the earth itself. They answered their questions about the lights with far more ghostly explanations.

The Inuit, who live in the frozen arctic wasteland see the northern lights frequently. They believed, and some still believe today, that the aurora borealis was the dancing spirits of people who had all been killed at once—for example, villagers who had been attacked by invaders. They remained inside their igloos when the lights filled the sky. They feared that if the spirits saw them, they might pick them up to join in their sky dance.

Imagine yourself bundled in clothing made of sealskin and furs, visiting the land that lies so far north that the ground is frozen solid and trees cannot grow: the land on the coast of the Arctic Ocean, on top of the world. There is nothing like an arctic winter to chill the bones. Temperatures average well below zero, frequently falling to minus 50 degrees Fahrenheit. Now, it is not easy to survive here, and you had best have a guide, let's say a friendly Inuit woman named Pipaluk. Pipaluk and the other Inuit in the village are experts at surviving in this, one of the harshest environment on earth.

The Inuit must work hard to stay alive. In winter, the only natural resources they have to sustain their bodies, build their homes, and make their tools and clothing are snow, stone, animal skins, meat, fish, and bones. At the time we are visiting the Inuit, they live in snow houses called igloos. An igloo has an entrance, an annex for storage, and a living area. Several people live in one igloo. These homes are known for being friendly, happy, relatively warm places (the average temperature inside an igloo is 40 degrees Fahrenheit). Here family members are especially careful to be kind to one another and respect each other's privacy, despite the somewhat cramped quarters.

Wintertime is seal hunting season. The hunters must walk out onto the frozen Arctic Ocean and search for the breathing holes of seals. Even though seals swim in the sea, they are mammals and, like whales and dolphins, must come up for air. They chew distinct holes in the ice in order to do this. It is through these holes that the patient hunters, who wait for hours at a time, finally spear the seal through its head when it pokes its nose up to breathe. This may sound cruel, but seal meat is a staple in the diet of the Inuit, who live where one cannot grow vegetables or raise cattle and other grazing animals. The Inuit kill these animals only when they must and only in order to survive. Their existence depends on the continued survival of seals in the ecosystem.

Inuit use not only the meat of the animals killed, but also their skins and furs for clothing and the tusks and bones to make hunting tools. One such tool is the *ulu*, an incredibly versatile knife used for nearly everything, including cutting chunks of ice.

The hunters must be constantly alert and listen for even the slightest noise that might indicate that the ice is cracking. Sometimes large chunks of ice break from the mass and float rapidly out to sea as ice floes. A person stranded on an ice floe would be in deadly danger.

Inuit play some interesting games, for example, a ball game called "Those Who Crowd Together." Everyone playing has a partner, and the object of the game is for one pair of partners to throw the ball back and forth to each other while the rest of the players try to get the ball away from them. The balls are made from animal skins sewn together with hide. The Inuit chew on a strip of hide to soften it and make it into a flexible thread. People have a lot of fun playing this game as they run, slip, slide, and fall in the snow.

Another Inuit game is called "Those Who Play at Dying." Inuit life is difficult and challenging. Starvation is a constant threat. Inuit children witness many funerals. The dying game reflects this fact. One child lies in the snow, and the other children build a snow wall around him. The rest of the children stand around this wall, weeping and wailing. This is the way people are buried and mourned in the land where the trees end.

Inuit have a wonderful way of solving disputes between grown-ups. The people involved in the dispute do not yell or physically fight. Instead they engage in a special duel—a song duel! The entire village gathers in the council house igloo, and the two people involved in the dispute stand in the middle and sing insults at one another. The winner, judged by the response of the listeners, is the one who comes up with the smartest, funniest insults!

At the end of the day, the Inuit gather inside their igloos and light whale oil lamps for light and warmth. Often they lie under their fur blankets as a storyteller like Pipaluk tells a tale. Many stories are told while the aurora borealis dances in the sky, for the Inuit will not venture out of their igloos until these lights go away.

Spirits of the Dancing Dead

The villagers looked up in awe and amazement at the night sky. The giant curtain shimmered in iridescent greens and blues. Akla, the village shaman, commanded all of the people to go inside their igloos. "Do not come out until morning!" he insisted. Even the dogs were placed in the igloo annexes.

Inside the igloos, surrounded by the flickering light from whale blubber oil, the people removed their warm clothes and huddled under the fur skins of their beds on the igloo floor. In hushed tones, the elders told the young ones what was happening.

"The *arsharshar* is in the skies. These are the spirits of the dead—perhaps they died from hunger. If they see you, they will surround you and lift you up into the skies with them!"

Sixteen-year-old Tatque's two younger brothers lay huddled under the covers, very frightened. Tatque was more concerned with the little orphaned pup in their igloo's annex. Its mother had been killed and eaten by a hungry polar bear several days ago. The pup still had a gash on its leg. Tatque got up from bed and wrapped herself in a fur. She went into the annex and lifted the little pup, carrying him back into the family bed with her. He was shivering, and, as she warmed him, she sang him a lullaby.

All living things must survive.
Bear ate your mother,
You are alive.
I will be your mother now.
Pup, pup, sleep.
Pup, pup, sleep.

Tatque's mother spoke to her, "Sometimes I think all you care about are those dogs."

"Not so, Mother. Most of the time, my thoughts are for Keok!" Not only was Keok the handsomest young man in the village, he was the kindest. He always had a smile for everyone and encouraging words for the elders whose joints ached with the cold.

Upon hearing Tatque's words, her father spoke. "You'd best put all thoughts of Keok out of your mind. Akla, the shaman, has demanded you as his wife. He is powerful. To disobey him could mean death. Tatque, I am

---

sorry, but for the sake of our family, you will have to accept Akla as your husband."

Tatque cried herself to sleep. Her sad parents cried with her in their hearts. The spirits of the aurora borealis danced overhead.

No one had counted on Keok's reaction to Akla's demand for Tatque. He simply would not hear of it! "Tatque, I am yours, and you are mine! I will challenge Akla to a song duel. The winner shall take you as wife. I promise that I will be the winner!"

The villagers, anticipating an exciting duel, gathered in the council house. Akla was the last to arrive. He was furious that his demand for Tatque was being challenged. A bully who often abused his powers as shaman, Akla was used to getting his own way. Keok stood tall and proud. "My love for Tatque, and hers for me, is stronger than your evil magic!" he declared. Because Akla was the eldest and, of course, the shaman, he began the duel. He was so angry at having been challenged that he could think of nothing to sing except "Keok, Keok, Keok is a, a, fool." The villagers waited. Finally, something came to him:

> *Keok sounds like kayak.*
> *Keok is a boat.*
> *That's why he's so stupid.*
> *His silly brains just float!*

A ripple of laughter was heard from the villagers. Now it was Keok's turn:

> *Akla is our shaman,*
> *And that is a true shame.*
> *Shamans have great powers.*
> *Akla's powers are lame.*

The people had to think about this one, then laughed happily. Akla continued

> *Keok thinks he's handsome.*
> *He thinks he's really nice.*
> *His heart's so very warm,*
> *It will melt his igloo's ice!*

From *Day of the Moon Shadow: Tales with Ancient Answers to Scientific Questions.*
©1995. Libraries Unlimited. (800) 237-6124.

The villagers roared with laughter at this one. It appeared that Akla was in the lead. Keok took a deep breath and sang

Akla's nose is so long,
Much longer than his toes.
It cuts right through his igloo
And leaves holes in his clothes!

The villagers laughed heartily. This was the best insult yet. Akla covered his nose and said, "You can't do that! You can't say that! There's nothing wrong with my nose." He was so upset at Keok's insult that his head went blank. He could think of nothing to sing except

Keok is, is, Keok, Keok is—
A walrus! Keok is, Keok is—

Akla's time was up, and again it was Keok's turn:

Akla's brains are floating.
All he can do is squeal,
And bark, and clap his hands.
Akla is a seal!

The villagers roared with laughter now. It was evident that Keok was the winner. Tatque ran to him. The two embraced. Akla, livid with rage and jealousy, stormed away to plan his revenge on the young man who had humiliated him and the young woman who rejected him.

That night the *arsharshar* appeared once again, and the villagers retired early. The lights in the sky seemed even more sinister, for the villagers feared Akla and what he might do because of his defeat. Their fears were real, for the vengeful man had crept into the annex of Tatque's igloo, stolen the little orphaned pup, and hidden it. Now he sat in his igloo conjuring up a spell. He concentrated on the vision of Tatque sitting in her igloo. With this image in his head, he sent evil waves through the air. Then he channeled his spirit voice to Tatque's igloo, and with it, made sounds of a pup scratching and whining outside.

Akla's spell on Tatque began to work. She went outside in search of the pup. The evil spirit voice moved toward the shore and out onto the ice. Tatque followed the compelling sound, walking farther and farther on the ice. Under Akla's spell, she forgot that it was now spring, and with the weather warming up, ice floes breaking away were a constant threat. A thunderous crash echoed through the air as the lights of the *arsharshar* hovered in the night sky above. A huge chunk of ice broke away, carrying Tatque with it. She yelled and screamed for help, but the villagers could neither see nor hear her as they huddled in their igloos to keep from being abducted by the dancing spirits in the sky above.

Tatque, thinking she would simply find the pup and bring him inside the igloo, had not dressed in her warm clothing. By morning she would certainly freeze to death. On a distant ice floe she noticed a polar bear. Like the other people in her village, she had learned to make the sounds of the animals, to speak their language in order to call them near so they could be hunted. Tatque called, "Rrraarrr" (please, help me). "Rrraarrr, rrraarrr" (I will die if I do not return to my village!).

The polar bear recognized Tatque's voice and understood her plea. Immediately, he dove into the icy waters to swim to her, remembering how the dogs of her village had spread word of her kindness to animals. The big, white, furry creature reached the ice floe that carried Tatque. He pushed and pushed, trying to force it back toward the shore, but the current against him was too strong. He called on the walrus and seal to help him. Hearing his cry, they quickly came to his assistance. The three animals used every bit of strength that they could muster but were unable to push the floe back to shore against the pull of the strong current.

They paused to think, then discussed this dreadful predicament. Unanimously, they decided there was only one solution. They must call for supernatural help. They looked up at the dancing spirits of the *arsharshar,* and each, in his own language, beseeched these awesome spirits for help.

RRRahrr RRRahrr RRRahrr RRRahrr
Spirits, help us.
Tatque must not die!

Bark! Bark! Bark! Bark!
Spirits, help us.
Hear us in the sky!
Bark! Bark! Bark! Bark! Bark!

Wee-uu-oh! Wee-uu-oh! Wee-uu-oh!
Spirits, hear us,
Hear our pleading cry.

From *Day of the Moon Shadow: Tales with Ancient Answers to Scientific Questions.*
©1995. Libraries Unlimited. (800) 237-6124.

The aurora borealis wavered and dipped its fireworks of gold and silver, whooshing and exploding in the sky overhead. As the trio pleaded for help, Tatque's father realized that his daughter had been gone far too long. He ran to Keok's igloo. "I fear the spirits have lifted my daughter into the sky!"

"I fear this is Akla's evil magic!" Keok replied. He ran to Akla's igloo. "Where is she?" he demanded.

Akla pointed toward the sea. "Go find her, brave lover! Then the two of you will be captured by the sea forever! Ha!"

Keok ran to the shore and called for Tatque, but to no avail. He leaped into his kayak, determined to find his beloved, but he had no idea in which direction she had floated. Frightened and confused, he forgot entirely about the *arsharshar* dancing above his head until, suddenly, he was surrounded by shimmering, colorful lights. The spirits descended from the heavens, singing in breathy tones while they danced and chanted about him

> *OH OH ee-ee-oh-oh*
> *Ah-ha ya-ha-ha-ha*
> *Oo-oo-yoo yai-yai-yai*
> *Ha-ha-ha-ha-ha-ha-ha-ha*
> *Yan-gai-yan-gai yai-yai*
> *Woo-woo woo woo-gee*
> *Woo-woo woo woo-gee*
> *Ah-ha ah-ha yai*
> *Oh-ho oh-ho ho*
> *Ya-ya ya-ga-wa ya*
> *Ya ya ya-ga-wa ya*
> *Ya-ga-wa ya-ga-wa yai-yai wa*
> *Yai yai ya-ga-wa ya-yai!*

The spirits lifted Keok into the sky. He fought them, but their powers greatly exceeded his, and he was forced to succumb to their whims. However, up as high as the spirits took him, he could see far and wide. Quickly, he scanned the sea, and there, to the north, he saw Tatque on her ice floe, huddled next to the polar bear to keep warm. "Please!" he cried. "I must save Tatque!"

Keok felt himself falling, whirring through the cold night air. Certain he would fall to a crashing death, he was stunned and amazed to find that he

---

had landed gently in a snowdrift. The spirits danced around him, saying, "Go, go, go, go, go to Tatque, Tatque, Tatque," and returned his kayak to him.

He climbed in and paddled frantically until he reached the ice floe. Keok thanked the animals for protecting his beloved. He wrapped Tatque in a fur, hugged her, and lifted her into the kayak. With the help of the polar bear, seal, and walrus, he was able to paddle this remarkably agile little boat through the currents of the icy sea and back to the shore near the village.

When they finally reached shore and said grateful good-byes to the animals, an unearthly crash resonated through the air. It sounded like multitudinous ice floes breaking away, each with its own supply of sky thunder. Terrified, the villagers ran out to see what was happening. There, surrounding Akla's igloo, were the Spirits of the Dancing Dead, leaping, twirling, bending, twisting, and chanting their powerful song

Wa wa wa wa!
Yan-ga wa!
Ha! Ha!
Wa oo oo oo wa!
Yan-ga-wa-wa yai yan-ga-wa!

They lifted Akla and his igloo into the air, higher and higher. Then, from a great height, they let it go. Their laughter echoed as the igloo fell to the ground, smashing into pieces and burying Akla amid the chunks of ice. The villagers attempted to dig him out, but they could not find him. Casting their eyes on a strange object sticking out of the snow, they approached it and cautiously began to dig around it. Here, they found Akla! The strange object turned out to be—his nose! The spirits had cast their magic on Akla. His nose now reached far out in front of him, a nose as long and blubbery as a seal's flipper! Keok's insult from the song duel had come true! Poor Akla, every which way he turned, and every time he turned every which way, he banged his nose into someone or something.

The spirits removed Akla's magic powers and granted them to Keok, who became a wise and revered shaman. The next day, the villagers celebrated when Keok took Tatque as his wife. Forever after, they lived happily together! To this day, it is said that, on nights when the spirits of the *arsharshar*, the aurora borealis, dance in the heavens, three visitors can be seen going into Keok and Tatque's igloo: a polar bear, a seal, and a walrus.

RRRahrr RRRahrr RRRahrr RRRahrr!
Spirits helped us.
Tatque did not die!

Bark! Bark! Bark! Bark!
Spirits helped us.
Heard us in the sky!
Bark! Bark! Bark! Bark!

Weeuuoh! Weeuuoh! Weeuuoh!
Spirits heard us,
Heard our pleading cry!

References

Science

- Asimov, Isaac. 1920. *Library of the Universe: The Sun*. Milwaukee, WS: Gareth Stevens.

- Chapman, Sydney. 1964. *Solar Plasma, Geomagnetism, and Aurora*. New York: Gordon & Breach.

- *Encyclopedia of Astronomy and Astrophysics*. 1989. San Diego: Academic Press, Harcourt Brace Jovanovich.

- Harre, Rom. 1981. *Great Scientific Experiments*. Oxford: Phaidon Press.

- Ley, Willie. 1962. *Life Nature Library: The Poles*. New York: Time Life.

- Souza, D. M. 1994. *Northern Lights*. Minneapolis, MN: Carolrhoda Books.

Anthropology

- *America's Fascinating Indian Heritage*. 1978. New York: Reader's Digest Association.

- Freuchen, Peter. 1961. *Book of the Eskimos*. New York: World Publishing.

- Martin, Patricia Miles. 1970. *Eskimos: People of Alaska*. New York: Parent's Magazine Press.

- Phebus, George. 1972. *Alaskan Eskimo Life in the 1890s as Sketched by Native Artists*. Washington, DC: Smithsonian Institution Press.

- Rasmussen, Knud. 1932. *Intellectual Culture of the Copper Eskimos*. New York: AMS Press.

- Viereck, Phillip. 1962. *Eskimo Island: A Story of the Bering Sea Hunters*. New York: John Day.

Folklore

- *Folklore, Mythology and Legend*. 1972. New York: Harper & Row.

- Millman, Lawrence, reteller. 1987. *A Kayak Full of Ghosts*. Santa Barbara, CA: Capra Press.

- *Tales of Eskimo Alaska*. 1971. Anchorage: Alaska Methodist University Press.

Music

- *An Anthology of North American Indian and Eskimo Music*. Folkways FE 4541.

- *Eskimo Songs from Alaska*. Folkways 4069.

- *Music of the Eskimos of Hudson Bay and Alaska*. Folkways FE 4444.

The Lullaby

From "Spirits of the Dancing Dead"

Music and Lyrics by
JUDY GAIL

Song Duel

From "Spirits of the Dancing Dead"
Page 1

Music and Lyrics by
JUDY GAIL

AKLA: ♩=92 Ad Libitum

voice

drum ostinato ... drum sempre ostinato

Ke- ok sounds like kay- ak. Ke- ok is a boat.

That's why he's so stu- pid. ___ His sil- ly brains just float!

KEOK:

Ak- la is our sha- man, ___ and that is a true shame.

Sha- mans have great pow- ers. ___ Ak- la's powers are lame!

AKLA:

Ke- ok thinks he's hand- some. ___ He thinks he's real- ly nice. His

heart's so ve- ry warm, ___ it will melt his ig- loo's ice!

Song Duel

From "Spirits of the Dancing Dead"
Page 2

KEOK: Ak- la's nose is so long, —— much long- er than his toes. It

cuts right through his ig- loo —— and leaves holes in his clothes!

AKLA: Ke- ok is—— is Ke- ok —— Ke- ok is —— a

SPOKEN:

wal- rus! Ke- ok is, —— Ke- ok is ——

KEOK: Ak- la's brains are float- ing. —— All he can do is squeal, and

bark, and clap his hands. —— Ak- la is a seal!

Song of the Animals

From "Spirits of the Dancing Dead"

Music and Lyrics by
JUDY GAIL

Verse 2 is sung at the end
of the story.

2. RRRahrr RRRahrr RRRahrr RRRahrr!
Spirits helped us.
Tatque did not die!

Bark! Bark! Bark! Bark!
Spirits helped us.
Heard us in the sky!
Bark! Bark! Bark! Bark!

Weeuuoh! Weeuuoh! Weeuuoh!
Spirits heard us,
Heard our pleading cry!

Song of the Spirits

From "Spirits of the Dancing Dead"

Music and Lyrics by
JUDY GAIL

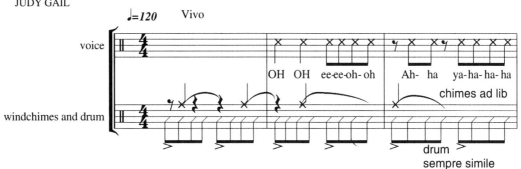

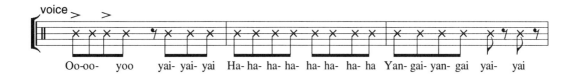

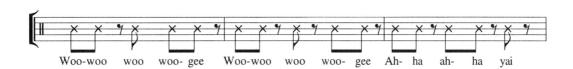

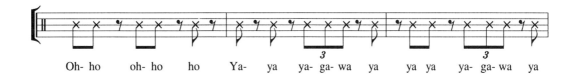

Chant of the Spirits for Akla

From "Spirits of the Dancing Dead"

Music and Lyrics by
JUDY GAIL

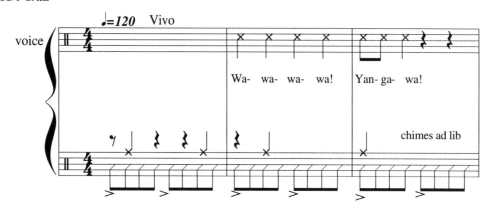

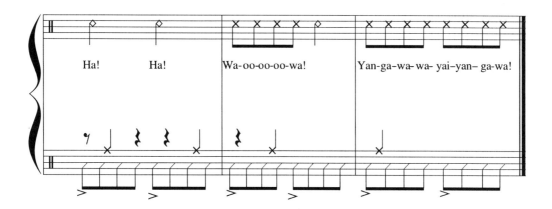

9

PELE'S REVENGE

A Story from Hawaii

What made the mountains and islands we know?
Were they formed out of lava from a hot volcano?
I wonder and ask, ask and wonder!

The continents as we know them today were not always where they are now. They are always moving, although extremely slowly. According to the theory of plate tectonics, the outer shell of the earth is made up of moving slabs or pieces called tectonic plates. Each of these plates makes up a portion of ocean or continental crust—the sand and rocks we step on while swimming, the mountains and valleys, and the land we walk and build our homes on. As these plates continue to move slowly and constantly, they sometimes move apart.

Many miles beneath the surface of the earth, a vast amount of heat energy remains stored in molten, or liquid, rock, called magma. When this magma meets a weakness in the earth's crust (an area where the plates of the crust have parted), it breaks through to the surface, resulting in a volcano. Beneath the earth's crust and above the magma is a rigid mantle of rock. Magma is held in place by the tremendous pressure of this rock. However, because it is lighter in weight than the rock, the magma, like weeds pushing through cracks in a sidewalk, works its way up through the slightest fissures, or cracks, in the rocks.

Besides molten rock, the magma also contains gases. As magma rises, its gases, always in motion, dissolve and expand with such great force that, eventually, they blast a hole through the earth's crust. The magma then pours out, carrying dust and ash into the sky and flowing over the ground.

There are different types of volcanoes. In some, magma flows freely to the surface of the earth, where it rapidly travels down any incline. Then the magma, called lava when it emerges above the earth's crust, cools and hardens into a solid. This type of volcano is often active for centuries without sudden, devastating eruptions.

In other volcanoes, where the magma is more like sticky taffy candy, the cooling lava piles up and forms steep-sided cones. As long as magma flows freely and consistently, the powerful forces

159

beneath the earth's crust are safely released. But sometimes lava hardens above the huge area containing the magma and blocks it. Over many years, the pressure of the blocked magma builds up. When it finally erupts, it can cause huge clouds of ash, dust, and pumice (a lightweight, glassy rock) that fill the air and cover the land, choking and suffocating people and animals.

There are about 850 active volcanoes on earth. About 214 of these are under the oceans, most in an area called the Ring of Fire, which arcs from New Zealand north along the eastern edge of the Pacific Ocean to the Bering Sea and Alaska, then south along the Pacific coast of North America and South America.

Some volcanoes, like those that formed the Hawaiian Islands, do not erupt where the earth's plates separate. Volcanoes such as these are created by hot spots, where magma rises from a fixed place in the earth's rocky mantle. Plate tectonics cause the earth's crust to drift over these hot spots. The crust can be compared to a lid on a pot of boiling water, where the pressure of the gases escaping from the boiling water forces the lid upwards. Similarly, the pressure of the magma gases builds up under the earth's crust, causing an eruption. This eruption forces the earth's crust to rise, often breaking the surface of the ocean, forming new islands. As the earth's plate continues moving over the hot spot, it erupts again and again, creating a chain of islands all originating from a single hot spot.

Volcanoes can cause much destruction. Sometimes, when a volcano's cone collapses or the volcano shifts the earth's tectonic plates, it can cause tsunamis, or tidal waves, as much as 1,000 feet tall. However, volcanos also have positive results. Volcanoes are responsible for some of the richest, most fertile soil on our planet. They are the makers of mountains and islands. Today, thanks to technological discoveries, the probability, though not the exact moment, of a volcanic eruption can be fairly accurately predicted. Hundreds of years ago, this scientific knowledge did not exist—but volcanoes certainly did! When a volcanic eruption occurred, what did people think caused this incredible spewing forth of fire into the sky?

The great explosions of fire and lava appeared mysterious and frightening to ancient peoples, who attributed these happenings to angry gods and goddesses. The ancient Romans believed that the god Vulcan was a blacksmith who, when angered, heated so many metals to such a hot temperature that the melting metal and sparks of fire poured down on the earth and its people as punishment. Some of the volcanoes on the Hawaiian Islands are inactive or silent at present. Others, like Mauna Kea, Mauna Loa, and Kilauea, are constantly erupting. The Polynesians, or ancient Hawaiians, believed that a goddess ruled over volcanoes. Her name was Pele, and she had a bad temper. Before learning more about Pele, imagine yourself in ancient Hawaii, long before the days of modern, high-rise hotels, tourists, and automobiles.

See the huts made of grass? There is a large one in the center of the others. That one belongs to the king. Then you see a man with a feathered headdress—a high priest. Walking around the village, the high priest talks to the people. Notice that every time he comes close to someone, that person immediately sits down on the ground and bows their head until the high priest leaves. Only after he leaves will the person get up and return to work or other activities. What has the high priest been saying to the villagers?

"Beware! King Kemana is coming! Observe the *kapus!*" *Kapu* is the Hawaiian word for taboo—or something forbidden for religious reasons. In ancient Hawaii, anyone not obeying taboos would be killed on the spot! When King Kemana arrives, the people must lie face down and not dare to get up—or look up—until the king leaves. They must also make absolutely sure that the king's shadow does not touch their bodies! When the king comes, all the people fling themselves on the ground. If we follow the king, we might see the high priest helping him into a boat. Once he leaves, everyone can get up from the ground and resume their normal activities.

Kapus, or taboos, were part of the religious laws established to protect *mana*, or spiritual power. The Hawaiian king was believed to be a god on earth and had great *mana*. If something common came in contact with the king, then his *mana* would be lost, and the gods would be angered. No one on the island could be safe when the gods were angry! The ancient Hawaiians took these taboos so seriously that they made *kapu* sticks. These were symbols that meant "Stay away! Forbidden!" There were *kapu* sticks in front of the king's hut. There were also *kapu* sticks in front of pools of drinking water, to make sure no one bathed in the water meant for drinking. Many *kapus* were established for people's safety. Anyone violating a *kapu* was killed on the spot and offered to the god Ku!

The ancient Hawaiians obeyed the *kapus* strictly. They also enjoyed many pleasures like singing, music, laughter, and succulent foods such as a whole pig roasted in a fire in the ground, then smothered with rich sauces made from fruits found on the islands. They played a variety of games and competed in sports of their own creation—including sledding matches! Obviously, there was no snow in this tropical climate; the natives of the islands built large wooden sleds and glided down big hills covered with smooth pebbles and grass. The Hawaiians viewed someone who was extremely fat as being absolutely exquisite. To them, a 300-pound king or queen was to be admired!

These ancient people had their own answers about volcanoes. They lived surrounded by them and on land formed by volcanic eruptions. The Hawaiians believed that Pele, the goddess of volcanoes, lived in the Kilauea crater on the big island of Hawaii. Pele became extremely hot-headed when angered. She stamped her foot in rage, and the volcanoes responded by erupting and pouring hot lava on the villages and their inhabitants, scorching everything in their wake.

Sometimes Pele would visit villages disguised as a young woman and play games with people. She would never tell anyone who she really was. This was most dangerous, for if Pele did not win the games, her fury caused her to literally blow her top, enveloping the winners in hot lava and turning them forever into statues. Pele also changed her appearance at times to that of an old woman, usually right before a volcano erupted. People were very cautious if they saw an old woman they did not know walking through the village.

Imagine now that it is the day of the great Makahiki, the feast celebrating the harvest of crops such as breadfruit, coconuts, bananas, yams, mountain apples, and taro, from which they made poi. Musicians are playing drums and flutes. Dancers bend and sway to the rhythms of the music and the songs and chants of singers. Pigs have been slaughtered and are roasting in earth pits. Fruits and coconuts decorate the tables, where happy people eat, talk, laugh, and listen to stories told by animated tellers.

Pele's Revenge

The Makahiki stars, the Pleiades, had been seen in the sky for the first time that year. This signaled the villagers that it was time for the harvest to begin. They looked forward to feasting, dancing, and singing to celebrate. There would be no work now, and certainly no war. Instead, thanks would be given to Lono, god of the harvest!

We sing happy praises upon this Makahiki.
Praises to Lono, who grows in all things.
Praises to Lono, who visits in the rain clouds,
Which water our earth from which our food springs.

Lono our god, our god of peace and farming.
Lono our god, the harvest will bring.
In this Makahiki, we celebrate so happily,
And give thanks to Lono, to Lono we sing!

The people were excited about something else, too: It was time for the great sledding race! Everyone busily greased the big wooden sleds with kukui nut oil to help them slide down the big grassy hills. For the past four years, the king had been the winner. Oh, did the people love their king! He was six feet, two inches tall and weighed 375 pounds.

Two children in the village, Kimo and his sister, Iollana, were particularly excited, for they were given the honor of maintaining the king's *holua* slide. They had to make sure that the round pebbles lining the hillside were covered with grass. The race was about to begin. The king would race against Mahkey, the high priest. The two lifted their sleds to the countdown—5, 4, 3, 2, 1, 0! They flung themselves on their sleds!

Lightning, flesh, and blubber fly
On the king's holua slide.
Sleds all greased with kukui nut oil,
Who will flip and who will glide?
Who will flip and who will glide
On the king's holua slide?
On the king's holua slide,
Who will puff his chest with pride?

The king won for the fifth year in a row! Everyone cheered. Mahkey picked up his sled and was about to leave when a young woman wearing a colorful skirt walked up to him and challenged him to a race! Mahkey was frightened. What if she, a woman, won? He would become the laughingstock of the village. Yet, he had to accept her challenge, for village rules stated clearly that one must always be kind and generous to a stranger—even if that stranger happened to be a woman! However, Mahkey quickly formed a plot in his mind. Politely he said, "Young woman, I will be happy to grease your sled."

The young woman accepted his kind offer. Mahkey put the oil of the kukui nuts on the bottom of his sled. However, while the young woman looked around at the magnificent view from the hilltop, he put water on the bottom of her sled. Young Kimo and Iollana, looking forward to watching the race, saw what Mahkey did. They could not believe that a high priest would be so deceitful. They wanted to tell a grown-up—but that was *kapu*! Two common-ers could not speak out against a high priest—particularly two children! No one would believe them, and worse, they would violate a *kapu* and be killed!

The race began. Mahkey's sled went flying down the hill at lightning speed. The woman's sled stopped and started, started and stopped! Natu-rally, Mahkey won the race. Without a word or even a glance at her opponent, the young woman picked up her sled and angrily stormed out of the village. As she did, she passed Kimo and Iollana, who were frightened by her eyes. In them they saw raging fires! They suspected that this was Pele, goddess of volcanoes. They knew for certain when they heard the words she sang as she left the village:

> *I am Pele, goddess of volcanoes.*
> *No one dares to make me look like a fool.*
> *Fool indeed! I'll show them in one flash,*
> *When I cover them with searing hot lava and ash.*
>
> *Mauna Loa, heat up all your embers.*
> *Fires burn, and molten liquid churn!*
> *Belch out boiling liquid, smoke, hot ash, and lava.*
> *Mauna Loa, I'll win this race—now it is my turn!*

Kimo and Iollana were scared. They turned to look toward Mauna Loa and saw a small plume of steam rise from its crater. They felt the earth quake slightly under their feet. The villagers' voices rang with songs of celebration. Kimo and Iollana realized that it was up to them to save the village! Both children had heard that sometimes Pele would accept a peace offering of delicious ohelo berries dropped into the crater of Kilauea, her home. They ran to their grass hut and grabbed gourds to fill, then hurried to the edge of the forest to pick the berries. There was not a moment to waste.

> *Pick ohelo berries, offer them to Pele.*
> *Drop them into Kilauea. Hurry now, we can't delay.*
> *Pele loves ohelo berries. It's said they work a charm.*
> *If we give ohelo berries, she might not do us harm.*

When the gourds were full, they ran to Kilauea. Slowly and painstakingly, the two children hiked up the dangerous terrain, working their way toward the top. Hot, out of breath, hearts beating with fear, they dropped the berries by handfuls into the crater. A loud noise and a burst of thick black smoke sent their hearts racing. There, right before them, Pele appeared!

"Why do you throw these berries into my home? I do not want your berries!"

"Please take them! " Kimo pleaded.

"Please," Iollana cried, "Kimo and I saw what Mahkey, the high priest, did to your sled. Please do not let Mauna Loa erupt and destroy our village just because of him! Accept our berries as a peace offering!"

"I do not want your berries! I, a goddess, have been cheated—humiliated before all of your villagers! I can never face them again. They must go, not I! Mauna Loa will indeed erupt. Look! Look how her steam hisses and the molten lava begins its flow!"

"Please, Pele!" Iollana cried. "Would you kill 100 innocent villagers for the act of one foolish bully?"

There is love in our village,
In our village there is love.
Is your pride more important than love?
In all living things, as the heart beats and sings,
Pride can destroy, but love more love brings.

Would you kill a mother as she rocks her little baby?
Or kill a young boy as he carves a doll for his friend?
Would you drown the father teaching his son to swim the waters?
Or make the widowed grandma suffer more sad crying?

There is love in our village,
In our village there is love.
Is your pride more important than love?
In all living things as the heart beats and sings,
Pride can destroy, but love more love brings.

"Oh, well, oh, Iollana," Pele tried to stifle her tears. "That is indeed a touching song. OK, OK! You have calmed my anger. However, there is a problem. There is only one way to stop a volcano from erupting once it has begun. That way is through a sacrifice! The sacrifice of a human heart! Are you, Kimo, or you, Iollana, willing to offer your heart to save your village?"

From *Day of the Moon Shadow: Tales with Ancient Answers to Scientific Questions.*
©1995. Libraries Unlimited. (800) 237-6124.

The two children were utterly terrified and could neither move nor speak for several minutes.

"Well, Iollana," Pele laughed. "Where is your love now? And you, Kimo, where is your great bravery?"

Kimo and Iollana quickly realized that the survival of their village depended solely and wholly on them. Both spoke at once, "I will sacrifice my heart!"

"Very well," Pele answered. "There is no time to waste. Mauna Loa is steaming great streams of smoke and ash. We must get there immediately." With a swing of her hand she transported them to its peak. As they looked toward their village beyond, they witnessed the flash of lightning and the booming echoes of thunder. The earth trembled and quaked, and the shrieks of terrified villagers reached their ears. Black smoke enveloped and choked Kimo and Iollana, and their feet burned from the intense heat of the ground beneath them.

As they approached the rim of the great crater itself, Kimo thought, "I will jump in and sacrifice my heart and life to save my sister." Iollana decided, "I will jump in and give my heart to save my brother." Pele leaped on a rock and chanted

Great Mauna Loa, great Mauna Loa,
Mauna Loa, Mauna Loa, Mauna Loa, Mauna Loa.
Great Mauna Loa, I will quench your desire.
Here's a human heart if you will stop your fire!

Great Mauna Loa, great Mauna Loa,
Mauna Loa, Mauna Loa, Mauna Loa, Mauna Loa.
Great Mauna Loa, eat the heart and let it end!
Be at peace with the children of men!

Mauna Loa, Mauna Loa, Mauna Loa, Mauna Loa!
Mauna Loa, Mauna Loa, Mauna Loa, Mauna Loa!

"Now it is time for the sacrifice! Kimo—or Iollana—jump!"

Both children, each wishing to save the other, jumped into the crater of the volcano. They swirled and twirled through the thick black smoke and heat that enveloped them, waiting to be sucked up forever in the molten rock. Suddenly, all the heat turned cool! Blackness transformed into vivid greens and gentle blues. Instead of melting rock, Kimo and Iollana felt sand beneath them, the silky, cushioned sand of the beach surrounding their village! Opening their eyes, they turned around to see Pele standing before them once more.

"Mauna Loa could not take the hearts of children so brave, honest, and kind as the two of you! Do not fear, Mauna Loa will find its own sacrifice. Look upon it, my children, do you see how the lava is rolling back up and into the crater? The steam, too? Go now! Go and celebrate the great Makahiki feast. But before you go, let me thank you."

> *I give my thanks to Kimo and to you, Iollana.*
> *I give these thanks to you upon this very day.*
> *You taught me, a goddess, a most important lesson.*
> *You taught me how to love and put my foolish pride away.*

(Note: sung to the tune of "Song of the Makahiki")

From *Day of the Moon Shadow: Tales with Ancient Answers to Scientific Questions.*
©1995. Libraries Unlimited. (800) 237-6124.

"Run along now! Go join your villagers and their feast. Leave Mauna Loa to me!"

As the two ran toward the festivities, the earth trembled to the vibrations of a crashing noise. The villagers shrieked once more as they gazed in awe at Mauna Loa, but the volcano did not erupt. Instead, facing toward the gigantic crater, a statue appeared—a statue carved not by human hands, but by lava! There, facing Mauna Loa, stood the high priest Mahkey, hardened forever, as solidly as stone! Pele had indeed found her revenge—and Mauna Loa its sacrifice!

Kimo and Iollana looked at each other. They knew that because of *kapus* they must carry their secret within and between themselves and only themselves forever. Quietly, they sang

> *We sing thanks to Pele, our goddess of volcanoes.*
> *We sing thanks to Pele, who kept danger away.*
> *We sing thanks to Pele upon this Makahiki,*
> *Here, in our village, we sing thanks to her today.*

(Note: sung to the tune of "Song of the Makahiki")

From *Day of the Moon Shadow: Tales with Ancient Answers to Scientific Questions.*
©1995. Libraries Unlimited. (800) 237-6124.

References

Science

- Carpenter, Allan. 1991. *The Encyclopedia of the Far West*. New York: Facts on File.

- Gregory, K. J. 1990. *The Earth's Natural Forces*. New York: Oxford University Press.

- Harris, Stephen L. 1990. *Agents of Chaos: Earthquakes, Volcanoes and Other Natural Disasters*. Missoula, MT: Mountain Press.

- *Planet Earth*. 1982. Alexandria, VA: Time Life.

- Witfield, Phillip, ed. 1990. *Atlas of Earth Mysteries*. Chicago: Rand McNally.

Anthropology

- Anderson, Rufus. 1964. *The Hawaiian Islands: Their Progress and Conditions*. Boston: Gould and Lincoln.

- Bailey, Paul Dayton. 1975. *The Kings and Queens of Old Hawaii: A Mele to Their Memory*. Los Angeles: Westernlore Books

- Chickering, William H. 1941. *Within the Sound of These Waves*. New York: Harcourt Brace Jovanovich.

- Clark, Sydney. 1950. *All the Best in Hawaii*. New York: Dodd, Mead.

- Feher, Joseph. 1969. *Hawaii: A Pictoral History*. Honolulu: Bishop Museum Press.

- Frazer, James G. 1981. *The Golden Bough: The Roots of Religion and Folklore*. Reprint. New York: Avenel Books.

- Henry, Marguerite. 1946. *Hawaii in Story and Pictures*. Chicago: A. Whitman.

- Smith, Bradford. 1957. *The Islands of Hawaii*. Philadelphia: J. B. Lippincott.

- Whitson, Skip, comp. 1976. *Hawaii-Nei, The Kingdom of Hawaii, 100 Years Ago*. Albuquerque, NM: Sun.

- Williams, Julie Steward. *Kamehameha*. 1985. Honolulu: Kamehameha Schools.

Folklore

- Westervelt, W. D., reteller. 1987. *Myths and Legends of Hawaii: Ancient Lore*. (Tales of the Pacific). Honolulu: Mutual.

- Williams, Julie Steward. 1985. *Pele and Volcanoes*. Honolulu: Kamehameha Schools.

Music

- *Hawaiian Chants, Hulas and Love Dances*. Folkways, 4271.

- Webly, Edwards. *Hawaii Calls: Favorite Instruments of the Hawaiian Islands*. Capitol Records, DN-1617.

Song of the Makahiki

From "Pele's Revenge"
Page 1

Music and Lyrics by
JUDY GAIL

Song of the Makahiki

From "Pele's Revenge"
Page 2

which our food springs. Lo- no our god, our god of peace and farm- ing. Lo- no our god, the har- vest will bring. In this Ma- ka- hi- ki, we cel- e- brate so hap- pi- ly, and give thanks to Lo- no, to Lo- no we sing!

Reprise

Sung by Pele

I give my thanks to Kimo and to you, Iollana.
I give these thanks to you upon this very day.
You taught me a, a goddess, a most important lesson.
You taught me how to love and put my foolish pride away.

Sung by Kimo and Iollana

We sing thanks to Pele, our goddess of volcanoes.
We sing thanks to Pele, who kept danger away.
We sing thanks to Pele upon this Makahiki.
Here, in our village, we sing thanks to her today.

Sledding Song

From "Pele's Revenge"

Music and Lyrics by
JUDY GAIL

Pele's Song of Anger

From "Pele's Revenge"
Page 1

Music and Lyrics by
JUDY GAIL

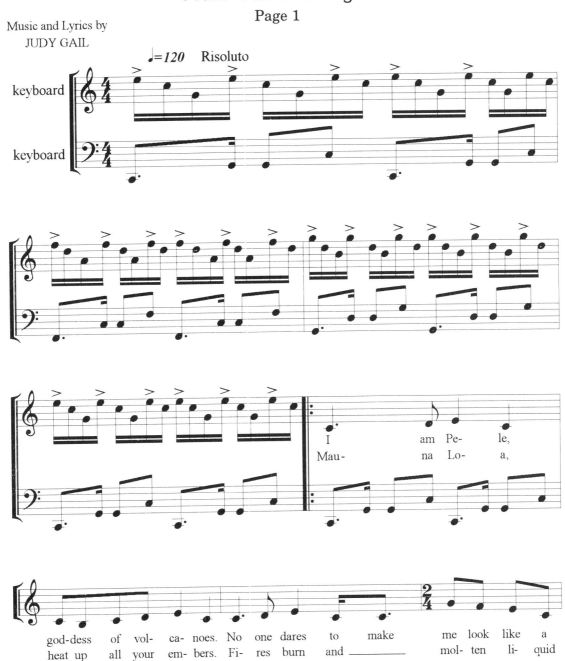

I am Pe- le,
Mau- na Lo- a,

god-dess of vol- ca- noes. No one dares to make me look like a
heat up all your em- bers. Fi- res burn and _____ mol- ten li- quid

Pele's Song of Anger

From "Pele's Revenge"
Page 2

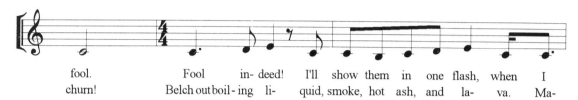

fool.   Fool   in- deed!   I'll   show them   in   one flash,   when   I
churn!   Belch out boil- ing li- quid, smoke, hot   ash,   and   la- va.   Ma-

cover them   with sear- ing hot   la- va and   ash.
u- na   Loa,   I'll win this race-- now it is my

turn!

Pick Ohelo Berries

From "Pele's Revenge"

Music and Lyrics by
JUDY GAIL

Pick o- he- lo ber- ries, of- fer them to Pe- le.

Drop them in- to Ki- la- u- e- a. Hur- ry now, we

can't de- lay _____. Pe- le loves o- he- lo ber- ries. It's

said they work a charm. If we give o-

he- lo ber- ries, she might not do us harm.

Iollana's Song

From "Pele's Revenge"

Music and Lyrics by
JUDY GAIL

Pele's Chant

From "Pele's Revenge"

Page 1

Music and Lyrics by
JUDY GAIL

♩=126 Con fuoco

cymbals, bongos, conga

accomp. sempre simile

Great Ma- u- na Lo- a,   great Ma- u- a Lo- a, Ma- u- na

Lo- a, Ma-u- na Lo- a, Ma- u- na Lo- a, Ma- u- na Lo- a, cresc. ----------

1.

Great Ma- u- na Lo- a, I will quench your de- sire.

Here's a hu-man heart if you will stop your fire!

2.

Great Ma- u- na Lo- a, eat the heart and let it end!

to coda

Be at peace with the chil- dren of men!

tambourine

Pele's Chant

From "Pele's Revenge"
Page 2

10
THE BLIND MAN AND
THE DEAF MAN

The Blind Man and the Deaf Man

A Story from India

How do our senses tell us and show
All the things in the world that we have to know?
I wonder and ask, ask and wonder!

Imagine not being able to smell anything. You would not know if there was a fire in your house because you could not smell the smoke. You would not be able to tell if you smelled of sweat and needed a bath. You would not be able to tell if the milk in your cereal was sour—and you would not be able to taste it either, because if you cannot smell, you cannot taste! Smell and taste are called the twin senses because they work so closely together. Try putting on a blindfold and holding your nose. Have someone give you a piece of food. Chew it and see if you can tell what you are eating. Chances are, you will guess wrong—even if it is a strong onion! Even something as strong-smelling and -tasting as an onion cannot be tasted if you cannot smell!

Our senses of taste, touch, sight, hearing, and smell teach us all we must know about the outside world in order to learn to protect ourselves. Our bodies have a system of nerves called receptors. The things we touch, smell, taste, see, or hear excite these receptors and signal them that we are eating something too hot, just right, cold, bitter, or sweet; touching something sharp, rough, smooth, hot, or cold; seeing a bear in the woods, a beautiful tree, a dark thundercloud; hearing Mozart, heavy metal, a siren screeching, the telephone ringing; smelling rancid cottage cheese, pleasant perfume, food frying, smoke burning, or chlorine in the swimming pool. In this way, our bodies are like an electrical circuit. The stimulus we touch, taste, and so on, acts as the switch that turns on our receptors. The receptors then send signals to the brain. The brain sorts out the information, saying, "Stop the car for the red light!" "That's a piano I hear playing." "What delicious chocolate I'm eating!" "Ouch! That's hot!" Or "Phew! What a nasty smell!"

There are times when one or more senses are damaged through birth defects, from disease, or through an accident. What happens when some senses do not work and are handicapped? The other senses compensate, or help out, and become stronger.

For example, one day a girl said to a friend of hers who was blind, "That's a nice yellow shirt you have on."

"Yellow?" her blind friend responded. "Yellow means nothing to me. What does mean something to me is the soft, cool way this shirt feels on my skin." He then told her, "There is an advantage to being blind. You make friends according to how nice a person is—you just sense this—without being influenced by how bad- or good-looking they might be!"

This same friend loved to dance. When asked how he knew where to move without bumping into others, he answered, "Because I cannot see, my ears have learned to tell me where objects and people are. The sound of the music bounces off everything around me, telling me whether the sound is close or far away. Because of this, I know whether the people and objects are close to me or at a safe distance. I can also feel whether something is close through my skin. I feel the heat or cold, or vibration of the object or person."

Deaf people cannot hear and do not know what music sounds like. However, when a train rumbles by, a jet roars above, or a band is beating its drums, plunking its guitars, and blowing its horns, they can feel vibrations through their bodies. They can also see to read lips and speak in a special sign language.

In most countries today, handicapped or disabled people are respected, given employment, and recognized as full human beings. In the past, many cultures around the world feared and rejected handicapped people and forced them to live as outcasts or beggars. Some cultures looked on handicapped people with awe and reverence, believing that the gods had blessed these people with special powers.

In the Asian country of India, the country that Christopher Columbus was actually looking for when he landed in America and mistakenly called the native people there "Indians," the holy men teach that there are five gateways to the mind: the hands, to touch; the nose, to smell; the eyes, to see; the ears, to hear; and the mouth, to taste. Through these gateways pass all the feelings and knowledge that enlighten the mind. Through discipline, special exercises, and consistent meditation, they believe one can cultivate a sixth and higher sense that imparts knowledge and wisdom beyond the five senses.

Use your senses now to visit India, an exciting land with mountains, rolling plains, blistering deserts, calm lakes, and fertile shorelines. Most of the millions of people who inhabit India are farmers, but India also has many large, crowded cities like Bombay, New Delhi, and Calcutta. In India, some people are extremely wealthy, but most are very poor. Monsoons, typhoons, droughts, and earthquakes plague the land from time to time. These disasters often ruin farmland, forcing farmers to leave their land and move to cities. Jobs are not easy to find, and many farmers cannot read. It is a common sight in large cities to see whole families cooking, eating, and sleeping on the streets amid shops and markets.

Streets in these cities are jammed with a strange mixture of traffic: cars, trucks, bicycles, jitneys pulled by men, carts drawn by horses and camels—and people riding elephants! Climb on an elephant to ride through India's beautiful countryside—or board a jam-packed train. Do not expect a seat. Some people are even riding on top of the train. Hope you are near a window and can stick your head out for fresh air. The windows are all open, for it is exceedingly hot, and you will not find air-conditioning. The breathtaking scenery should distract you as it draws you into its beauty.

See the great and sacred Ganges River as you ride along its banks. Indians believe that bathing in this river washes away all earthly sins. They come from miles away on pilgrimages simply to bathe in the holy waters of the Ganges. Look at the farming villages with their little mud huts and roofs made of straw. These huts have no running water, thus no showers, toilets, bathtubs, or sinks. If you wish to wash or have to go to the toilet, you do so along the village river. The only furniture in the hut is a bed made from wood and ropes, no mattress.

In this village, people do not use money. When they need to buy something, they use the barter system. For example, someone might trade a pair of sandals and a piece of cloth for a pot of milk and a cup of rice. A farmer might give several pounds of rice as rent to the landlord who owns the land where the farmer plants. If the farmer owns the land, he might give rice he has grown to pay for other types of seeds to plant.

In this village, you will not find any meat to eat, for many people are of the Hindu religion and are vegetarians. To them, cows are sacred, and these animals roam villages and cities to be fed by those who worship them. Killing any animal is unthinkable—even a cockroach! There is a reason for this.

In the Western world with its Judeo-Christian culture, it is believed that time goes straight forward. There is a past, a present, and a future. When a moment is gone, it is gone forever. In India, the Hindus believe time is a revolving circle without beginning or end. Anything that has happened will happen again. Anything that has not already happened will never happen. People are born and die over and again, returning in different forms. This circular, never-ending cycle of death and rebirth is called reincarnation. How a person acts in this life determines what kind of form they will have in the next life. If you are really good in this life, you may come back in the next life more intelligent or wealthy or even as a revered holy man. If you are not so good in this life, you could come back as a donkey or a rat. If you are really bad, you could come back as a cockroach. That is why you do not want to step on a cockroach. It might have the soul of an ancestor!

To the Hindus, the body is like a suit of clothes. As we discard clothes when they are worn out, so the soul discards the worn-out body and puts on a new body. These bodies are the vehicles that take our souls through life, helping us to learn and grow. For the Hindus, if a person is handicapped, it is not a catastrophe. Evidently, something happened to that person in a former life, and the handicap is now being used as a teaching tool to help that person prepare for a better next life. To the Hindus, there is one universal truth or spirit—the cosmos. All people, all animals, all things are part of this cosmos. Therefore, even if a person is lacking one of the five senses, true knowledge is not hidden from them because truth is not found in the world of our senses. Truth comes from the cosmos and, thus, can be found only in our souls.

Imagine yourself in the city of New Delhi. You are at a gala festival. The streets are teeming with people. You feel the hot sun beating down on your skin, smell the delicious odors of spicy curried foods cooking, hear musical instruments playing and people singing, and see throngs of people dancing and bumping into one another on the crowded streets. Then you encounter a storyteller telling this tale.

The Blind Man and the Deaf Man

One day at a festivity of music and dancing called a *nautch*, a man turned to the man next to him and said, "I think this music is wonderful, but I don't care much for the dancing. I am blind. I can't see."

The man sitting next to the blind man watched his lips carefully as he spoke. Then he answered, "Quite the contrary. I think the dancing is marvelous, but I don't care much for the music. I can't hear. I am deaf." The deaf man then added, "Truthfully, I don't understand how you can know the world at all. Why, you wouldn't know a bird from an elephant!"

"How wrong you are," the blind man replied, and he sang

I am a blind man and I cannot see.
Yet I know the world and what it can be.
I know the world through ev'rything I touch,
I know the world through ev'rything I smell.
I know the world through ev'rything I taste upon my tongue.
I know the world through ev'rything I hear.
Vibrations around me,
Waves trav'ling to me.
My ears have eyes.
The light travels through me.
Ah om ah om.

Making sure to mouth his words clearly, the blind man said, "Truthfully, I don't understand how you can know the world. Without hearing, you cannot know the song of the bird from the bellow of the elephant. You live in a world of silence cut off from communication!"

The deaf man stepped close to the blind man and said, "How wrong you are!" And he sang

I am a deaf man, and I cannot hear.
Yet, I know the world with my body so dear.
My eyes can see things no hearing man can see.
My fingers can feel things no man who hears can feel.
My tongue, it tingles with every drop of food I taste.
My nose, it tells me what's good and what is waste.

From *Day of the Moon Shadow: Tales with Ancient Answers to Scientific Questions.*
©1995. Libraries Unlimited. (800) 237-6124.

Vibrations around me,
Waves trav'ling to me.
My eyes have ears. The sound travels through me.
Ah om ah om.

"I tell you what," the blind man said. "You be my eyes, and I'll be your ears. That way we'll both learn more of the world!"

The two walked off toward the forest together. The deaf man said he knew of a shack where they could live. On the way, the blind man heard the braying of an abandoned donkey. With the blind man following its sounds, and the deaf man leading his blind friend through the woods, the two found the braying animal. On the donkey's back was a *chatee*, a large, round ceramic pot. The deaf man said, "We are very lucky. We shall have a shack, a donkey, and a *chatee*!" Soon the deaf man said, "Stop! I have found some juicy black ants. They will make a very interesting sight to passersby in our shack." He put the ants into a silver snuff box and put the box into his pocket. The two walked on slowly, for the donkey was hungry and stopped to eat every dry patch of grass he could find.

Hee-haw, I am a donkey.
They say I'm very dumb.
My old master has whipped me.
Thank goodness that he's gone.
These two seem very gentle,
Though one sees and one hears.
I may be a dumb donkey,
But I've got eyes and ears!
Hee-haw hee-haw hee-haw.
Hee-haw hee-haw hee-haw.

Suddenly, the deaf man screamed as he saw a lightning bolt flash before his eyes. "Help! We must get out of here before this lightning burns us up!" Then the forest echoed with a thunderous sound. The blind man wailed, "Oh, no! I don't see that lightning is so bad, but this thunder is awful! We must find shelter."

The deaf man looked around. In the distance, he saw a beautiful house and led the blind man and the donkey to it. The deaf man knocked on the door. The blind man heard no answer. He groped with his hands until he found the door knob. He turned it, and the door opened. The two men and the donkey went inside. Not a soul was within. The deaf man's eyes nearly popped out of his head in amazement as he gazed on a room filled with gold coins and jewels. He led the blind man to a pile of these dazzling riches and told him to touch them. The blind man did as the deaf man said. As his fingers felt the round, cool coins and shapes of the jewels, and his ears heard the clinking sound of these coins and gems dropping back into their pile, he was overwhelmed with joy.

Cobwebs covered nearly every corner of every room, and the house looked as though the owner had been gone a long, long time. No one had come to claim the treasure. Thus, the two men felt free to pack up as many sacks of coins and jewels as possible. They loaded them on the donkey's back and prepared to leave as soon as the storm subsided. The deaf man locked and bolted the door and put the chain across it—and none too quickly!

A knock and booming voice shattered their joy: "Who has locked me out of my own house?"

Not having heard one sound, the deaf man had no idea what was going on. The blind man let him know. The deaf man then lifted the latch on the door but kept the chain connected. He opened the door and began to tremble uncontrollably as his eyes saw the intruder. It was an evil Rakshasa! He was a sickening blue color. He looked like a vicious dog standing on its hind legs. He had fangs the size of elephant tusks! Something told the deaf man that the blind man should not know about this. Not to see would be not to know. Not to know would be not to be afraid. At least one of them could remain calm this way. The deaf man could not stop shaking from head to toe as thoughts of the Rakshasa swirled through his mind.

> *Rakshasas disturb men at their prayers.*
> *Rakshasas haunt cemeteries.*
> *Rakshasas enter men through their food*
> *And sicken them like rotten berries!*
> *Rakshasas' fingernails are poisonous.*
> *Rakshasas are yellow, green, or blue.*
> *Rakshasas make mincemeat of humans and their flesh,*
> *And then they eat them, it's true!*

The Rakshasa knocked again. "I am a Rakshasa!" His voice was not quite as frightening as his appearance. The blind man was still not scared, and he answered, "Do not disturb us! If you do, I will punish you!" A plan to confuse the Rakshasa rushed through his thoughts, and before he knew it, he found himself saying, "I am Bakshasa! Bakshasa is Rakshasa's father!"

The slow-witted Rakshasa was indeed confused. "Bakshasa is Rakshasa's father? I didn't know that Bakshasa is Rakshasa's father!"

"Well, I am. And I am fierce!"

Bakshasa is fiercer than Rakshasa!
Bakshasa has far more power!
And if Rakshasa does not obey,
Bakshasa will kill him in one hour!

"OK, my father, Bakshasa. You've given me one hour. In that hour I want to see what you look like!"

The blind man mouthed these words for the deaf man. The deaf man thought quickly. He pulled the donkey toward the door and pushed its head through the opening under the chain.

"Ughhh!" The Rakshasa nearly choked. "How very horrible my father Bakshasa's face is! Now I want to see Bakshasa's body!"

Again, the blind man let the deaf man know what had been said. The deaf man thought quickly again. He took the *chatee* off the donkey's back and rolled it along the floor past the opening in the door.

The Rakshasa gazed on this big, round piece of clay. He gasped. "Truthfully, my father's body is much bigger than mine. Truthfully, my father could eat me up entirely. I better get out of here! But before I go, Bakshasa, I want to hear your terrible roar!"

Again the blind man mouthed what had been said for the deaf man. Quickly, the deaf man pulled the snuff box filled with the ants he had collected out of his pocket. He put the ants into the donkey's ears. The ants bit, tickled, and pinched the poor critter, and he let out a loud "HEE-HAAAAWWWW!"

"Ooohhhh!" the Rakshasa cried. "My father's voice would make even the most evil Rakshasa obedient. I better get out of here!" And the Rakshasa ran away.

The deaf man removed the ants from the donkey's ears and put them back into the snuff box. The next morning, the two men and the donkey left for the forest, unaware that the Rakshasa, still curious and totally confused, wanting to see Bakshasa, his father, in full daylight and full view, had waited behind a bush. When he saw the two men and the donkey and realized how he had been fooled, he grew furious. He sought the help of six evil Rakshasa friends and plotted with them to kill the blind man, the deaf man, and the donkey, and, of course, to retrieve the treasure. As the seven Rakshasas waited for their prey, they chanted

Rakshasas mm mm mm mm mm mm.
Mm mm mm mm mm mm mm Rakshasas.
Mm mm mm mm mm mm mm mm mm evil ones.
Mm mm mm mm mm mm mm mm mm mm mm pois'nous ones
Mm mm mm mm mm mm monstrous ones.
Mm mm mm mm mm mm Raksahsas.
Mm mm mm mm mm mm mm mm mm mm mm mm mm mm
Rakshasa! Rakshasa!
Rakshasa! Rakshasa!

When the deaf man spotted the seven Rakshasas, he shook all over. He could barely walk for fear. He said to the blind man, "There are seven evil Rakshasas waiting to kill us. What can we do?"

The blind man gestured to the deaf man, "Find the highest tree you can see. Help me to climb up it as you climb up after me." The deaf man, wracked with fear, misunderstood the instructions and climbed up the tree first, leaving the blind man to grope with his hands, arms, and legs. The Rakshasas ran after the two men. The deaf man held out his hand to help the blind man. He pulled him to safety in the highest branch of the tree just as the Rakshasas reached the trunk at the bottom. Rakshasas are not good climbers. When the Rakshasa leader saw the men high up in the tree, he commanded the other Rakshasas to stand on each other's shoulders to make a ladder of their own and reach the men.

When the deaf man saw what they were doing, he screamed, "They're coming after us!" Shaking in terror, he could not control his hand, and he let go of the blind man's arm, which, until this moment, he had held tight as a tiger's jaw on its prey. The blind man slipped. He grabbed onto two protrusions that he thought were tree branches. They were not. They were the ears of the Rakshasa leader! The Rakshasa leader lost his balance and fell onto Rakshasa six, who fell onto Rakshasa five, who fell onto Rakshasa four, who fell onto Rakshasa three, who fell onto Rakshasa two, who fell, with all the rest, onto Rakshasa one. All of the Rakshasas now lay in a confused heap on the ground.

The blind man, still holding the Rakshasa's ears, had no idea where he was. The deaf man realized this and yelled, "Hold on even tighter, I'm coming to help you!" The blind man squeezed even harder on the Rakshasa's ears. The other Rakshasas ran away, bruised and confused. The Rakshasa leader was now terrified. In order to save his own blue skin and his ears, he knocked the blind man off his back and pulled with all his might to get the blind man's hands off his ears. Then he ran away as fast as a Rakshasa can run.

The deaf man approached the blind man. Happy and relieved, he said, "What a pair we are! You don't fear what you can't see, and, though I can't hear, you listen to me!" The two collected the donkey and their treasure. "You know, my friend," the deaf man continued, "I think we should use our treasure to open a shelter where all those who are missing a sense can come—those

who can't touch, those who can't hear or see, those who can't taste or smell. Together, we shall combine our senses and, thus, know more of the world!"

"What a noble idea, my friend," the blind man replied. "Yet, never forget that truth lies beyond our mere senses, existing in all things within the cosmos! Let us strengthen our sixth sense and sit under the tree and meditate." As they meditated, with the blind man hearing and the deaf man seeing, the two chanted

> *Ah om ah om ah om ah om*
> *Ah om ah om ah om ah om.*
> *Vibrations around me,*
> *Waves trav'ling to me.*
> *My ears have eyes.*
> *The light travels through me.*
> *My eyes have ears.*
> *The sound travels through me.*
> *Ah om ah om ah om ah om ah.*

From *Day of the Moon Shadow: Tales with Ancient Answers to Scientific Questions.*
©1995. Libraries Unlimited. (800) 237-6124.

References

Science

- Harre, Rom. 1981. *Great Scientific Experiments*. Oxford: Phaidon Press.

- Martin, Paul D. 1984. *Messengers to the Brain: Our Fantastic Five Senses*. Washington, DC: National Geographic Society.

- Zim, Herbert Spencer. 1956. *Our Senses and How They Work*. New York: William Morrow.

Anthropology

- Brown, Joe David, ed. 1961. *India*. (Life World Library). New York: Time Life.

- Edwardes, Michael. 1969. *Everyday Life in Early India*. New York: Putnam.

- Maraes, F. R., and Robert Stimson. 1943. *Introduction to India*. London: Oxford University Press.

- Moore, Clark D., comp. 1970. *India, Yesterday and Today*. New York: Praeger.

- Stutley, Margaret. 1977. *Harper's Dictionary of Hinduism: Its Mythology, Folklore, Philosophy, Literature, and History*. New York: Harper & Row.

- *The Varieties of Sensory Experience: A Sourcebook in the Anthropology of the Senses*. 1991. Toronto: University of Toronto Press.

Folklore

- Haviland, Virginia. 1973. *Tales Told in India*. Boston: Little, Brown. ("The Blind Man and the Deaf Man" was inspired by the traditional tale, "Blind Man, Deaf Man, and Donkey" as found in this source.)

- Leach, Maria, and Jerome Fried, eds. 1950. *Standard Dictionary of Folklore, Mythology & Legend*. New York: Funk & Wagnalls.

- Narayan, Kirin. 1989. *Storytellers, Saints, and Scoundrels: Folk Narrative in Hindu Religious Teaching*. Philadelphia: University of Pennsylvania Press.

- Rugoff, Milton, ed. 1949. *A Harvest of World Folktales*. New York: Viking.

Music

- *Ragas from South India*. Folkways 31302.

- Shankar, Ravi. *Improvisations*. Los Angeles, CA: Ravi Shankar Music Circle, RSMC-6.

Vibrations

From "The Blind Man and the Deaf Man"
Page 1

Music and Lyrics by
JUDY GAIL

Vibrations

From "The Blind Man and the Deaf Man"
Page 2

VERSE 2. I am a deaf man, and I cannot hear.
Yet, I know the world with my body so dear.
My eyes can see things no hearing man can see.
My fingers can feel things no man who hears can feel.
My tongue, it tingles with every drop of food I taste.
My nose, it tells me what's good and what is waste.
Vibrations around me, waves trav'ling to me.
My eyes have ears. The sound travels through me.
Ah- om, ah- om.

The Donkey's Song

From "The Blind Man and the Deaf Man"

Music and Lyrics by
JUDY GAIL

Deaf Man's Song of Rakshasa Fear

From "The Blind Man and the Deaf Man"

Music and Lyrics by
JUDY GAIL

Bakshasa Is Fierce

From "The Blind Man and the Deaf Man"

Music and Lyrics by
JUDY GAIL

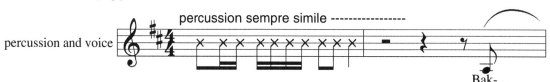

sha- sa is fierc- er than Rak- sha- sa! Bak- sha- sa has far more pow- er! And

if Rak- sha- sa does not o- bey, Bak- sha- sa will kill him in one hour!

Chant of the Rakshasas

From "The Blind Man and the Deaf Man"

Music and Lyrics by
JUDY GAIL

Vibrations Reprise

From "The Blind Man and the Deaf Man"

Page 1

Music and Lyrics by
JUDY GAIL

Vibrations Reprise

From "The Blind Man and the Deaf Man"
Page 2

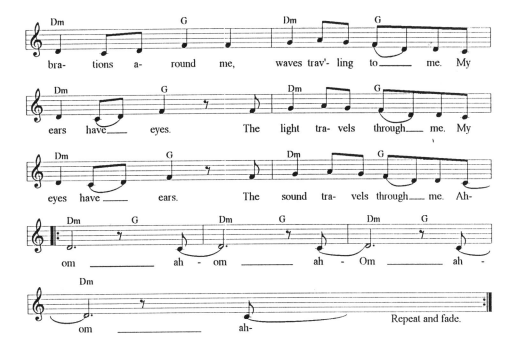

bra- tions a- round me, waves trav'- ling to____ me. My

ears have____ eyes. The light tra- vels through____ me. My

eyes have____ ears. The sound tra- vels through____ me. Ah-

om _____ ah - om _____ ah - Om _____ ah -

om _____ ah- Repeat and fade.

11
JOHN HENRY AND THE STEAM DRILL

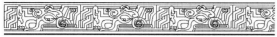 # JOHN HENRY AND THE STEAM DRILL

A Story from America

How did people come to know
How to invent machines and make engines go?
I wonder and ask, ask and wonder!

Human beings have brains that can wonder and question, seek answers and invent things, along with hands that can build. People have always searched for ways to make work easier, faster, and more efficient, to exert less effort to move a greater force: to gain a mechanical advantage. The following are five basic tools used to do this:

1. Cogs in wheels, or gears
2. Inclined plane, which was used to build the pyramids of Egypt
3. Pulleys, which make lifting heavy weights possible
4. Archimedes screw, an apparatus for raising water
5. Lever, a metal bar pivoted on a fixed fulcrum

A lever, for example, is a bar or board resting on a fulcrum—a center on which it can move up and down. By placing the bar or board over the fulcrum so that one end is longer than the other, we can lift a heavy weight, one that otherwise could not be lifted. Think of a seesaw with one end longer than the other. The lighter person sits on the longer side of the seesaw and thus has more leverage. Sitting on the shorter side, the lighter person would have a difficult time getting their playmate, the heavier person, up in the air.

If you try to lift a box filled with heavy items, you might not be able to do so, or it might be extremely difficult, tiresome, or even dangerous if you pull a muscle while trying. However, you can lift that box with a pulley. This simple device offers its mechanical advantage through the use of one or more small wheels. These wheels hang from a ceiling or another sturdy structure. The wheels have ridges in their centers, and ropes wind around these ridges. A hook is attached at one end of the rope and

203

then connected to the heavy object to be lifted. The end of rope hanging over the other side of the wheel is pulled, and the heavy weight is easily lifted.

Air can be used to offer a mechanical advantage. Air is made up of submicroscopic particles called molecules. These molecules vibrate and remain near to, but not always touching, one another. Blow up a balloon and hold it next to a pinwheel. Let the air out of the balloon. The pinwheel spins around because, when the air was blown into the balloon, it was compressed. Its loosely vibrating molecules were pushed close together—squashed into a small space. When released, the compressed, vibrating molecules created a power source. In the case of the balloon and the pinwheel, the compressed air molecules created enough energy to force the pinwheel to spin.

When a great deal of air is compressed, enough energy is produced to create electricity. If you continue to blow up the balloon, it will burst because the rubber from which the balloon is made is very thin. Imagine, however, that this air is blown into a non-bursting steel box. Now we are thinking along lines that can lead to an invention—and just such thoughts did!

In 1870, a machine called the steam drill was invented. Coal was used to start a fire that heated water until it boiled. Like air, steam can create power. The steam pushed a piston, a short cylinder, down into an air-filled cylindrical container. Through this motion, just as you blow air into a balloon, the piston pushed the air from the cylindrical container into a steel box. This process was repeated many, many times, until a tremendous amount of air was compressed or squashed into the steel box. The air then forced a valve to open at the other end of the box. Now the air pressed on a sharp steel drill, causing it to spin around and around. The drill, which could dig holes through rock, was used to create tunnels through mountainsides. Steam engine trains could whiz through these mountain tunnels and avoid having to go over the peaks. Until the steam drill was invented, men dug these tunnels by hand. The drill could do the work of 25 men at once!

Machines have made our lives easier and have enabled us to produce far more goods than we could without them. However, they have also made work more impersonal and have taken jobs away from people. The invention of machines and establishment of factories, known as the Industrial Revolution, caused a total change in peoples' lives. Today, every day, everyone relies on machines—air conditioners, heaters, alarm clocks, cars, televisions—the list goes on and on. Before the Industrial Revolution, life was much simpler, and people were responsible for their own survival. There were no supermarkets or shopping malls. Almost everything a family used and owned was made by that family's own hands. That meant that not only did they have to cook their food, but they had to hunt for it or grow it as well! They built their own houses with simple saws, hammers, and nails; crafted their own shoes; and sewed their own clothing by hand, without an electric sewing machine.

Imagine yourself in the state of West Virginia at the beginning of the Industrial Revolution. Go back to the year 1870, and hike to Big Bend Mountain Tunnel. You will see men building a railroad—laying track to go through the mountain's solid rock. They do not have a steam drill or any other machines that dig through rock, so they do it with their own hands. A man called a steel driver swings a huge, heavy hammer. Another man, called a shaker, holds a large metal peg. The steel driver hits the metal peg over and over, slowly chipping away at the rock until a hole is dug through it. The shaker prays for an accurate steel driver who will not miss the peg and hit him by mistake. When the hole is about seven feet deep, dynamite is put into the hole to blast the rock away. The men who do this hard labor often sing songs called work songs to help them keep a steady rhythm with their hammers.

Living on the American frontier was hard, hard work. Families lived far apart from their neighbors and had to face all kinds of dangers—from wild animals to sickness. These people still knew how to have a good time—even before television! Suppose a neighbor comes calling. He is a close neighbor—he only lives 20 miles away! He rides his horse or drives a horse-pulled cart, and when he arrives you sit on the front porch and swap tall tales. These tales are hilarious because the storyteller purposely exaggerates everything. For example, say you had an encounter with a mountain lion. Of course you were scared! When you tell the story, though, you might make the experience larger than life by saying that your mountain lion was not a normal 3-footer—no, sir-ee! He was 10 feet long and stood 8 feet high and had fangs the size of an elephant tusk, and he would have eaten your rifle—that is, if you were not the best darned sharpshooter in the land and had not shot him first!

Telling a tall tale like this is not easy, for the teller has to keep a perfectly straight face, even if the audience is laughing uproariously! Back then, a good tall tale was called "reckless, bamboozlin', tall tale-in', sky-paintin' oratory!" Tall tales helped people face their fears of wilderness dangers, for they made people laugh and described reality so ridiculously that, somehow, it did not seem as scary any more!

There is a tall tale about a real-life man named John Henry, a black man who worked as a free and paid man after the Civil War. John Henry helped to build the Big Bend Mountain Tunnel. He was a steel driver who could hammer deeper and faster than anyone. In real life, John Henry stood about 6 feet tall, but his reputation as a super steel driver had people calling him 20 feet tall in the many tales that were told about him.

During John Henry's life, the steam drill was invented. John Henry did not like that steam drill one bit! He was afraid that machines would take over the honest work men did with their hands, and, therefore, a man would have no way of making a living for his family. He challenged the steam drill to a contest. John Henry won that contest. According to legend, John Henry died from a heart attack right after he won the contest. In real life, however, most people who knew him claimed he actually died many years later, when a tunnel he was digging caved in. Whatever the true story is, John Henry is one of America's greatest, most beloved tall-tale folk heroes.

JOHN HENRY AND THE STEAM DRILL

It was a coal black night when the preacher rode up on his coal black horse to Ezra and Liza Henry's cabin. The lightnin' was a'flashin' and the thunder a'bangin', echoing through the mountain hills. Then all was still. Why, the sun comes out a'shinin'. At that precise moment, Baby John Henry was born. His first cry sounded more like the powerful cry of a grown man!

"Well a man ain't nothin' but a man!"

Preacher went over to the baby to give him his blessing. Soon as he's done, Baby John sings again

Thank you, preacher! I'm born, here I am!
I'm hungry, Mamma Liza,
Please bring me some ham!

Liza gave her baby some milk. After John had drunk one whole gallon, he sat up and said, "Mamma and Papa, I got to eats like I want. I got to eats like I should." Then, right before everyone's eyes, Baby John grew five inches in four minutes! Ezra, Liza, the preacher, and the midwife looked on in amazement. It was right then and there they knew that Baby John warn't no ordinary baby. He was a manchild! Then Baby John sang

Mamma, Papa, I is HUNGRY!
I wants four pounds of ham and hominy grits,
Seven little possums and twelve sweet 'taters!
Forty loaves of bread with lard,
Ten sides of bacon and twelve pig jowls!
Fourteen pots of black-eyed peas,
And some home-made ice cream!

You could hear his tummy a'grumblin'. Now Liza was angry that her baby didn't say please! She got out of bed and got some goofer dust. She put it into Baby John's ears. For a moment, he lay there in a stupor. Then he comes out of it and says

Please, Mama and Papa, I is HUNGRY!
I wants four pounds of ham and hominy grits,
Seven little possums and twelve sweet 'taters!
Forty loaves of bread with lard,

Ten sides of bacon and twelve pig jowls!
Fourteen pots of black-eyed peas,
And some homemade ice cream!

He even added, "Thank you." Well, after that, Liza never had to give him goofer dust again. Baby John was always polite and obedient. Overnight, Baby John grew to be nine feet tall! His muscles were strong as those of an ox. And his ears grew to be as big, yes, as big as a rabbit's! Next mornin', John Henry's sittin' on his papa's knee. Why, he was much bigger than his daddy, but Ezra said, "My baby is my baby. My baby done need my lovin' attention. My baby done need his pappy's knee!"

It was then that John Henry first set eyes upon his daddy's nine-pound hammer and the piece of steel lyin' next to it. He jumps right off his daddy's knee and sings

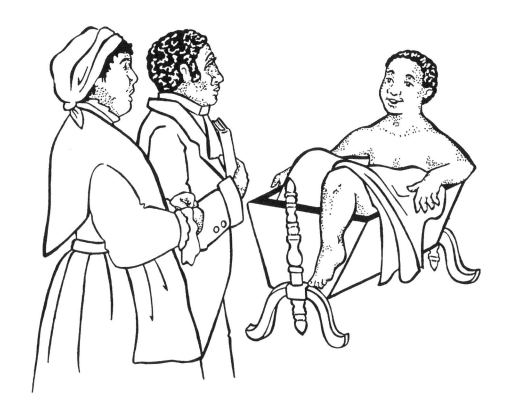

Pappy, oh my Pappy,
I know what my life will be.
This hammer and this piece of steel
Will raise the heat 'round me!

Then Baby John goes and picks up that hammer like he'd done it all his lifetime. Why, he picks it up powerful and straight and brings it down on the steel peg, makin' a hole in the ground that his daddy thought went clear through to China! John burst into song again!

Here's a nine-pound hammer
Swingin' in my hands.
I love to swing this hammer,
For my hands make me a man!

Well, John's voice boomed over the mountain hills and brought a visitor to the Henry yard to see what all was goin' on. She was big—six feet tall with big, handsome bones and a big, broad smile and a real big straw hat. Her name was Polly Ann. She took a likin' to John Henry—even though he was just a one-day-old baby. And John took a likin' to her. He said, "Polly Ann, you is goin' to be my wife! Mamma, Papa, when can I marry Miz Polly Ann?"

Ezra answered, "When you're three weeks old, Baby John. Yes, when you are three weeks old. Then you can marry Miz Polly Ann!"

Well, every day for the next two weeks, John went out into the yard a'hammerin'. Why, he grew to be 20 feet tall! His shoulders, they were as big as mountain boulders. Why, he could now lift one 20-pound hammer in his left hand and one 20-pound hammer in his right hand and swing them both down, hittin' the steel pegs with absolute precision! Now Baby John was goin' to get married in one week. He had to get a job! But he didn't have to go a'lookin'. The Henry cabin was near Big Bend, where they were building a tunnel right through the mountain rock so that new-fangled steam engine railroad could go through. Baby John's reputation had spread far and wide. One day there was a knock on the Henry cabin door.

"Is Baby John at home? Me name is Timothy MacDougal. I head the crew at the Big Bend Mountain Tunnel."

"Why, Baby John sure is here, Mr. MacDougal. But my baby sho' ain't no baby no mo'!" Ezra replied.

Baby John appeared. Mr. MacDougal nearly swallowed his tongue at the sight of him. "Me eyes have never seen anything like the wonder of it, Mr. and Mrs. Henry. Why, Baby John, would ye please work for me as a steel drivin' man startin' tomorrow mornin'? Will ye, John? I'll pay ye five times as much as the others, John."

"Sho', Mr. MacDougal!"

Next mornin' John started work. He teamed up with Li'l Willie. Li'l Willie was the best shaker on the railroad. He warn't no small 'un either. He stood seven feet, six inches high. Why, between him and John, the two of them nearly dug the whole Big Bend Mountain Tunnel. Li'l Willie was never afraid that John'd miss and hit him instead. John never missed, never, ever, never missed!

Well, next week John and Polly Ann was married. Every day that fine lady'd be right alongside John and Li'l Willie, singin' along with John and bringin' the two of 'em water whenever they were thirsty—and feedin' John whenever his tummy grumbled. All was goin' real fine, when one day a stranger come up the mountain and talked to Mr. MacDougal.

"Hello, my name is Splashy Waters and I've got the invention of the century! Why, my machine can do the work of 25 of your men, Mr. MacDougal. So why don't you buy my steam drill?"

"Mr. Water Splashin'—"

"That's Mr. Splashy Waters, if you please—"

"Mr. Splashy Waters, one of me men is far better than your machine. Why, me men are the best on the whole railroad!"

"Oh, yeah? Well, then, Mr. MacDougal, prove it! I challenge one of your men to a contest against my steam drill. Contest will be tomorrow from sunrise to sunset. Here's 500 dollars! Keep it—if you win!" And then he disappeared down the mountainside.

"John, John Henry! A man named Mr. Splashy Waters has challenged one of me men to a contest against his new machine—a steam drill, whatever that is! He says his one machine can do the work of 25 of me men! We'll show him, won't we, Johnny? Will ye be me man, John? Will ye?"

"Sho', Mr. MacDougal. I don't want no machine takin' over the work of my hands or the hands of any other man!"

Sunrise came. Mr. Splashy Waters and his crew were crankin' up that steam drill. She was a'hissin' and a'clankin'. Fire was spittin' right out of her rotary drill into the rock. John's voice could be heard singin' over all the noise of the machine. Polly Ann was right alongside him and Li'l Willie, singin' along with John, bringin' 'em water whenever they was thirsty, and, of course, feedin' John hog jowls and grits whenever his tummy grumbled.

We're diggin' down, down, down.
Gonna dig clear through to Mississippi,
Then dig clear through to China.
Gonna dig down, down, down.

"C'mon, John!"
Well, it's Li'l Willie cryin'.
"Burst that rock wide open,
Bust her clear, then dig inside!"

she breaks down. Hundreds of people ꟷ ee the contest. Mr. Splashy Waters was ꟷ ꟷis crew. "Fix it, you fools. Fix it! Why, the entire reputaꟷ ꟷtific Age rests on this here contest! Fix it, you fools!"

Meantime, John had finished diggin' one hole seven feet deep and started on another. The steam drill she broke down again! Mr. MacDougal laughed. "Hey, Mr. Splashy Waters, it takes more of yer men to get that steam drill goin' that it does fer me one man to be a'diggin'!"

John went right on.

> *"How am I doin', Li'l Willie?"*
> *"John, you couldn't be doin' fina!"*
> *"Willie, have we hit Mississippi yet?"*
> *"John, right now we're hittin' China!"*
> *Keep on diggin' down, down, down.*
> *Keep on diggin' down down down.*
> *Keep on diggin'.*

Just then, the sun disappeared over the mountains. That meant the contest was over. John Henry laid down his hammer. The crowd cheered. Mr. MacDougal waved the 500 dollars and said, "Ye did it! Ye did it, me Johnny! Ye proved that one man is worth far more than any new machine! John, ye dug two holes down, each 7 feet—that's 14 feet altogether! The steam drill she only dug one hole 9 feet!"

John Henry heard Mr. MacDougal's words and fell to his knees and lifted his hands to pray.

> *Love my hammer, love this land,*
> *Love my woman named Polly Ann.*
> *Lawd God Almighty, how I love these hands.*
> *I'm proud to be nothin' but a man!*
> *LAWD GOD ALMIGHTY!*

Then, John Henry fell to the ground with a thunderous crash! The baby manchild had done the work of a lifetime all in one day! And now, the baby manchild lay there on the ground, a dead old man. Everybody wept. They

---

From *Day of the Moon Shadow: Tales with Ancient Answers to Scientific Questions.*
©1995. Libraries Unlimited. (800) 237-6124.

buried John Henry in the Big Bend Mountain Tunnel, and every locomotive that goes roarin' by toots its whistle to say, "There lies a steel drivin' man!"

Then Polly Ann stood up tall and proud. "Now you all know that John wouldn't want us standin' around here cryin'. Why, in his short lifetime, he proved that a man ain't nothin' but a man. He proved that we all have a right to live! We all have a right to work! We all have a right to our dignity! Stand up, everybody! Raise yo' glorious hands, everybody! Let me hear you clap those beautiful hands, everybody, and sing along with me."

> *Love that hammer, and I love these hands!*
> *Ain't no creature in all the land*
> *With hands that do what our hands can do.*
> *Ain't no machine that's better than you!*
> *Clap! Clap your hands! Hallelujah!*
> *Shake, shake those hands! Hallelujah!*
> *Clap! Clap your hands! Hallelujah!*
> *Shake, shake those hands! Hallelujah!*

References

Science

- Horvatic, Anne. 1989. *Simple Machines*. New York: Dutton.

- Huntoon, Daniel T. V. 1877. *Oliver Smith Chapman—Steam Shovels*. Cambridge, MA: privately printed.

- *Illustrated Encyclopedia of Science*. 1984. New York: Exeter Books.

- Schulz, Charles M. 1981. *Charlie Brown's Fifth Super Book of Questions and Answers: About All Kinds of Things and How They Work!* New York: Random House.

- Singer, Charles; E. J. Homyrad; A. R. Hall; and Trevor I. Williams. 1978. *A History of Technology*. Oxford: Oxford University Press.

Anthropology

- Botkin, B. A., and Alvin F. Harlow. 1953. *A Treasury of Railroad Folklore*. New York: Crown.

- Dale, Henry; Rodney Dale; and Rebecca Weaver. 1992. *The Industrial Revolution*. New York: Oxford University Press.

- Daumas, Maurice, and Eileen B. Hennessy, trans. 1970. *A History of Technology and Inventions: Progress Through the Ages*. New York: Crown.

- Gorham, Michael. 1952. *The Real Book of American Tall Tales*. Garden City, NY: Franklin Watts.

- Lomax, Alan. 1960. *Folksongs of North America*. Garden City, NY: Doubleday.

Folklore

- Battle, Kemp P., comp. 1986. *Great American Folklore*. New York: Touchstone.

- Felton, Harold W. 1950. *John Henry and His Hammer*. New York: Alfred A. Knopf.

- Keats, Ezra Jack. 1965. *An American Legend*. New York: Pantheon Books.

- Killens, John Oliver. 1975. *A Man Ain't Nothin' But a Man: The Adventures of John Henry*. Boston: Little, Brown.

- Rugoff, Milton, ed. 1949. *A Harvest of World Folktales*. New York: Viking.

Music

- *Anthology of American Folkmusic*. Folkways 2951, 2952, 2953.

- "The Ballad of John Henry," in *Folksongs of North America*. Edited by Alan Lomax. Garden City, NY: Doubleday, 1960.

- *Brownie McGhee & Sonny Terry*. Folkways 2327.

- *Negro Prison Camp Worksongs*. Folkways 4475.

I'm Born, Here I Am!

From "John Henry and the Steam Drill"

Music and Lyrics by
JUDY GAIL

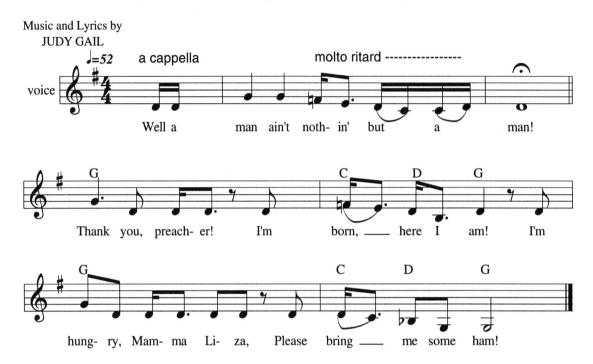

This song sounds good with the accompaniment of an actual organ or one simulated on an electronic keyboard.

I Is Hungry!

From "John Henry and the Steam Drill"

Music and Lyrics by
JUDY GAIL

To the accompaniment of a tambourine, this song should be half-sung, half-spoken much in the fashion and with the speed of an auctioneer.

Pappy, I Know What My Life Will Be

From "John Henry and the Steam Drill"

Music and Lyrics by
JUDY GAIL

Pap - py, — oh, my Pap - py, — I know what my life will be. This

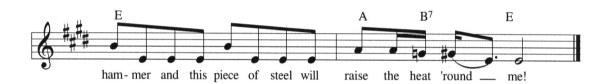

ham - mer and this piece of steel will raise the heat 'round — me!

This song is best accompanied by spoons, woodblocks, or hand claps.

Nine-Pound Hammer

From "John Henry and the Steam Drill"

Music and Lyrics by
JUDY GAIL

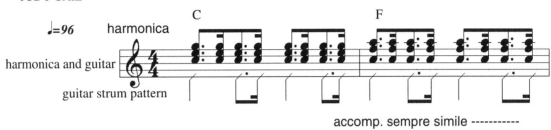

Here's a nine- pound ham- mer

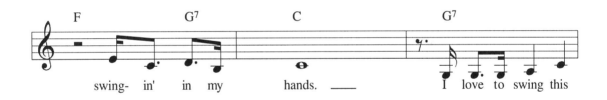

swing- in' in my hands. ____ I love to swing this

ham- mer, for my hands make me a man! _____

From *Day of the Moon Shadow: Tales with Ancient Answers to Scientific Questions.* ©1995. Libraries Unlimited. (800) 237-6124. Copyright ©1987, ©1995, Poppykettle Enterprises, Inc., Miami, Florida. (305) 387-3683. International copyrights secured. All rights reserved.

We're Diggin' Down, Down, Down

From "John Henry and the Steam Drill"

Music and Lyrics by
JUDY GAIL

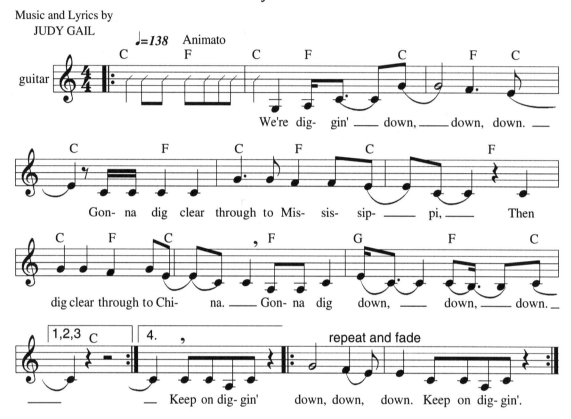

We're dig- gin' ___ down, ___ down, down. ___

Gon- na dig clear through to Mis- sis- sip- ___ pi, ___ Then

dig clear through to Chi- na. ___ Gon- na dig down, ___ down, ___ down. ___

___ ___ Keep on dig- gin' down, down, down. Keep on dig- gin'.

2. "C'mon, John!"
   Well, it's Li'l Willie cryin'.
   "Burst that rock wide open,
   "Bust her clear, then dig inside!"

3. "How am I doin', Li'l Willie?"
   "John, you couldn't be doin' fina!"
   "Willie, have we hit Mississippi yet?"
   "John, right now we're hittin' China!"

Each verse may modulate up a whole tone to help with the climax of the story line. Use the pivot chord (A7, then B7) on the 3rd beat of the last measure.

John's Prayer

From "John Henry and the Steam Drill"

Music and Lyrics by
JUDY GAIL

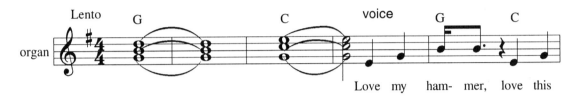

Love my ham- mer, love this

land, love my wo- man named Pol-__ ly __ Ann. Lawd God Al- might- y,

how I love these __ hands. __ I'm proud to be noth- in' but __ a __

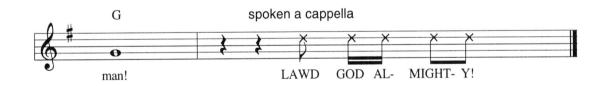

man! LAWD GOD AL- MIGHT- Y!

Love These Hands

From "John Henry and the Steam Drill"

Music and Lyrics by
JUDY GAIL

12
DAY OF THE MOON SHADOW

DAY OF THE MOON SHADOW

A Story of the Maya

How does the moon create an event that's atypical—
The solar eclipse, which is elliptical?
I wonder and ask, ask and wonder!

Imagine that it is a normal sunny day. Birds are singing, insects crawling, squirrels scurrying about. Suddenly, all of nature quiets! The sunny blue sky turns dark blue, then darker, and even darker. In the middle of the day you see stars in the sky! The sun slowly disappears until all that's left is a shimmering halo, thin as a pencil drawing of a circle. Where's the sun? What is happening? It is a solar eclipse.

The sun has a glowing, golden surface called its photosphere. This surface is not solid, but its density makes it impossible to see through as it produces nuclear reactions from within, creating temperatures of about 10,300 degrees Fahrenheit, or 5,700 degrees Celsius. Surrounding the photosphere is the corona, a thin layer of highly electrically charged, superhot gases. The corona is only one-millionth as bright as the photosphere and cannot be seen unless the photosphere is blocked from sight. This is just what happens during a total solar eclipse, and the moon is the cause of this extraordinary event.

The moon revolves around the earth, and the earth-moon pair revolve around the sun. The moon is 2,160 miles in diameter, and the sun's diameter is 412 times larger than that, but they appear to be the same size to someone standing on the surface of the earth. This optical illusion occurs because the sun's orbit is an average of 390 times farther away, and that tricks our eyes into seeeing the larger, more distant sun as about the same size in our heavens as the smaller, nearer moon. Sometimes, the orbits of the moon and the earth line up in a perfectly straight line with the sun. When this happens, the moon passes in front of the sun and blocks out the sun's rays, creating the magnificent spectacle of the solar eclipse and casting an elliptical shadow that moves rapidly across the earth's surface. As the moon moves between the sun and the earth, it appears as though a bite is being taken out of the sun. As more of the sun disappears, it looks as though it is being totally eaten up. Soon, all that is left is the shimmering, pencil-thin halo, or corona, which now can be seen as the photosphere is blocked from sight by the moon. Slowly, the sun begins to emerge again as the moon continues to move in its orbit. First, a small sliver of the sun becomes visible. Then a little more, then half, three-quarters, and more, until the entire sun appears again, and the corona disappears from our view once more.

The region of the earth where any total solar eclipse can be seen is less than 190 miles wide. In the area where the eclipse is total, or the sun is completely covered by the moon, the sky will darken. Stars will be visible. Some flowers close, and chickens and other birds roost. Eerie and strange colors paint the landscape and atmosphere. A total solar eclipse lasts 7.5 minutes at most. A larger area surrounding the path of the total eclipse falls under the partial shadow, or penumbra, of the moon. In this area, only a portion of the sun's disk is still visible, so the day dims but does not totally darken.

Today, scientists have created an array of instruments with which to study the sun and its corona. Through an instrument called a coronagraph, scientists can block out the photosphere and look at this amazing solar atmosphere. Telescopes and advanced mathematics have enabled astronomers and physicists to come up with explanations for what occurs during a solar eclipse.

Thousands of years ago, these facts were unknown. What did ancient peoples think when a solar eclipse occurred? Many were terrified, believing that a great dragon was eating the sun. They would bang on drums and shout, hoping to scare the dragon away. Naturally, they thought their noise worked because the sun always returned.

An exception were the Maya Indians, who lived in what today is the Yucatán Peninsula in Mexico and Guatemala in Central America. The Maya are recognized for their knowledgeable astronomers and mathematicians, who lived over 1,300 years ago! The Maya did not understand exactly what was happening during an eclipse because they did not know that the earth was a round planet with the moon orbiting it. However, they watched the heavens so carefully and took such precise and detailed notes that not only could they figure out when there would be an eclipse, but they could also predict the path of the planet Venus. Their astronomy was so accurate that they invented a calendar as good, if not better, than the one we use today.

Travel now to the city known today by the Toltec name of Chichén Itzá, located on the Yucatán Peninsula. Enter your imagination and visit this city in A.D. 1000, when it was known by its Maya name of Uuc-Yab-Nal. Changes are taking place, for the Toltec nation has invaded and brought new Toltec gods to replace older Maya gods. The Toltecs have also altered the Maya designs on their buildings. In the ceremonial center of the city live the ruler, his high priests, and their families. Farmer peasants live miles away in mud huts with thatched straw roofs. They grow all the food for the high priests and provide the labor to make the temples and palaces.

Why do the farmer peasants work so hard to support the royal family and priests in their luxury? One answer has to do with the astronomy and mathematics of the Maya priests. They are the ones who know how to read, observe the planets and stars, and calculate and predict eclipses and other celestial events. The peasant farmers, who cannot read, rely on the priests to tell them when to plant and harvest their corn, beans, and chili peppers and to give them the weather forecasts vital to successful farming. What would happen if the peasants decided to rebel? The priests would use their most powerful weapon against the peasants, their weapon of knowledge!

One of the most impressive ways the Maya priests used this weapon of knowledge was before and during a solar eclipse. The peasants believed that a rabbit, not dragon, would eat the sun. "If you don't obey us," the high priests would threaten, "we will tell the rabbit to eat the sun!" The eclipse would occur, and the peasants would do as the priests commanded. Some of these priests even used ventriloquism as a weapon. They would stand near clay statues in the images of the gods and speak without moving their lips in the same manner that you have seen ventriloquists with puppets. The amazed farmer peasants thought they were hearing the gods' voices and would do whatever the gods told them to do.

The Maya believed that the spirits of men helped the gods in their heavenly battles. Occasionally, they sacrificed people, many of whom wished to be offered to the gods, believing this was an honor and that they would reap great blessings in the afterlife. When the Toltecs invaded the city of Uuc-Yab-Nal, they insisted that Tezcatlipoca, the militaristic dread lord of the night, rule as king of the gods. Tezcatlipoca, they said, demanded that hundreds of humans be sacrificed to him. Maya storytellers told many tales of great battles between Tezcatlipoca and Kulkulkan, one of the Maya's more peaceful and kind gods. Kulkulkan usually demanded only a symbolic sacrifice of butterflies and flowers.

The Maya had a written language and told and wrote many tales of their lives and their gods. When the *conquistadors*, or Spanish conquerors, invaded, they destroyed virtually all of the Maya writings. Here is a tale that may be similar to ones told anciently about how a high priest of Kulkulkan used his knowledge of the stars to defeat a vile, high priest of Tezcatlipoca.

Day of the Moon Shadow

Ahcucumatz, high priest of the god Kulkulkan, god of wisdom, charity, and love, walked home to his palace rooms where he lived with his wife, Ix-Kalem, their three sons, and their daughter, Nicte. His heart was heavy with fear as he entered and saw his nine-year-old son, Zubac, marching around, pretending to be a Toltec soldier and chasing Nicte with a toy club. As he marched, Zubac sang

> *Beware, a Toltec soldier lives here,*
> *Soldier of adventure in life,*
> *Who, for his god, Tezcatlipoca,*
> *Trades, invades, and kills with his knife!*

Ahcucumatz reprimanded Zubac and thought, "How I hoped he would follow me into the priesthood and learn of the stars and mathematics like his two older brothers. But no, since the Toltecs have invaded, all he can think of is being one of them." He spoke to Ix-Kalem, "My wife, trouble has come to the city of Uuc-Yab-Nal. This god of the Toltecs, Tezcatlipoca, asks for human sacrifice—the sacrifice of little children. Yes, he asks for their hearts!"

"Why, Ahcucumatz, in our city an adult has been sacrificed occasionally—and willingly, wishing to bring a message to the gods, but a child? Never! Do not worry, the people will not allow this. Our god, Kulkulkan, will prevail, our god who asks for butterflies and flowers."

"I fear you are wrong, Ix-Kalem. The people are afraid not to obey. I was in the plaza, and with my own eyes and ears I saw and heard the god Tezcatlipoca speak. The high priests have a clay image, an idol of their god, and right from inside the clay, right from the idol itself, the voice of Tezcatlipoca poured out, saying, 'You are to obey my high priest, or you shall be destroyed!'"

The next day, the fear in Ahcucumatz's heart proved true. Toltec soldiers, led by the high priest of Tezcatlipoca, stormed into his palace home. The high priest had a terrible cold, and his sneezing and coughing momentarily interfered with his bullying. Ahcucumatz had no idea what he wanted, but terror seized him when the high priest grabbed Nicte and ordered his soldiers to tie her up.

"Ah-choo! You will see now which god is all powerful. Tomorrow night, your little daughter will provide our highest sacrifice. All the people will then obey us, for, if the daughter of the high priest of Kulkulkan goes to Tezcatlipoca, then so can all other children! Ah-choo!"

Ix-Kalem screamed, "Give me my daughter!" Despite her cries, the Toltec soldiers carried a terrified Nicte out the door. Ahcucumatz and his two eldest sons ran after them, trying to get her back, but they were helpless before the flashing knives and swinging clubs of the Toltecs.

After this horrible event, they left to go to the temple of Kulkulkan to pray and think. Little Zubac went to the central plaza, where a large crowd had gathered to stand before the clay idol of Tezcatlipoca. Zubac squeezed through the crowd and stood right up front. The idol began to sing. The high priest stood only a few feet away.

> *Oh, people of Uuc-Yab-Nal,*
> *Ah-choo! Ah-choo!*
> *Tomorrow night, one of my priests*
> *Ah-choo! Ah-choo!*
> *Will show you how very great I am.*
> *Ah-choo! Ah-choo!*
> *As he sends me the soul of one of your own,*
> *Ah-choo! You must do just as my priest commands,*
> *Ah-choo! for if you don't, you will all die, too!*
> *Ah-choo! Ah-choo! Ah-choo! Ah-choo!*
> *Ah-choo! Ah-choo! Ah-choo! Ah-choo! Ah-choo!*

Zubac had never heard the voice of a god before, and he did not know that gods could catch colds. He ran to the temple of Kulkulkan, where his father and brothers were still praying. "Father, Father! I just heard the voice of Tezcatlipoca. He kept sneezing, just like the high priest at our home. Can gods catch colds?"

"Zubac," Ahcucumatz asked, "was the high priest anywhere near the idol?"

"Yes, father, he was only a few feet away."

"Zubac, you have brought me an answer to a question I did not even ask. Gods cannot catch colds. The idol is not speaking. The high priest is! Somehow, he has learned to speak without moving his lips. This is not a

From *Day of the Moon Shadow: Tales with Ancient Answers to Scientific Questions.*
©1995. Libraries Unlimited. (800) 237-6124.

battle of power. It is a game of deceit. Two can play at this game. Oh, the timing could not be more perfect! My sons, tomorrow at high noon we are due for a total eclipse of the sun! We can use this knowledge to our advantage. Quick! Get out your instruments. Get our books. We must calculate the time of the eclipse exactly!"

Later, Ahcucumatz went to the palace of the high priest of Tezcatlipoca. "I come in the name of Kulkulkan, our god of charity, love, and wisdom. I challenge you to a contest of power. We will see whose god is greater!"

"Ah-choo! Oh, Ahcucumatz, this will be fun. We shall see you—ah-choo!—make such fools of yourselves! Ah-choo! Nicte shall be sacrificed tomorrow night! Ah-choo!"

The next morning, Ahcucumatz and his family went to the central plaza. Word had spread quickly, and thousands of people were there to witness this most important event. All heads turned as the high priests of Tezcatlipoca made their entrance. They walked and chanted two by two, each swinging vessels of smoking incense. Their colorful robes and huge feathered head-dresses dazzled the eyes of onlookers. The high priest of Tezcatlipoca led the procession as he carried the idol of the god. He passed Ahcucumatz, and, shoving the idol right up to his face, ventriloquized, "There is no way you can overcome our power. Tonight, Nicte dies. Ah-choo!"

The priests, with their backs to the crowd, then formed a circle. From within the circle, explosions and colorful smoke arose. Their voices rang through every corner of the plaza and seemed to vibrate from the trees, the air, and even the very ground as the priests chanted

Tezcatlipoca, god so very mighty.
Tezcatlipoca, god and lord of all the night!
Tezcatlipoca, bring the death to Kulkulkan.
Tezcatlipoca, let your mirror smoke and burn!

The people gazed and listened in awe and fear of the powers of this god. Meantime, Ahcucumatz looked toward his sons, who signaled him to begin talking.

"High priests of Tezcatlipoca, people of Uuc-Yab-Nal, I speak on behalf of the god Kulkulkan. Kulkulkan cannot abide such evil as practiced by Tezcatlipoca, a god of robbery and deceit. To stop the pollution of the evils spread by this god and his high priests, Kulkulkan will have to eat the sun and extinguish its flame forever!"

"Ah-choo! Oh, Ahcucumatz, this is even better than I thought. You know that no one controls the sun! Ah-choo!"

Ahcucumatz looked toward his eldest sons. They signaled that the eclipse was about to begin. Ahcucumatz began to pray

Kulkulkan, god of love,
Hear us pray, offering, from our hearts,
Butterflies as wond'rous as the skies.
Hear our hearts, filled with light,
And destroy the lord of night.

Someone screamed, then another, until all the people cried out in terror. Indeed, as they looked up, it appeared that the rabbit was eating the sun! As the sky grew darker, Ahcucumatz prayed louder

Kulkulkan, god of love,
You ask for gifts from the heart.
Kulkulkan, Tezcatlipoca, he asks
Only for the heart.
Hear our hearts filled with light,
And destroy the lord of night!

Now, even the priests of Tezcatlipoca were screaming. The high priest cried, "Ah-choo! Oh, Ahcucumatz, do something, do something. Talk to Kulkulkan! I don't want to—ah-choo!—die!"

From *Day of the Moon Shadow: Tales with Ancient Answers to Scientific Questions.*
©1995. Libraries Unlimited. (800) 237-6124.

"Get Nicte! Bring my daughter to me and stop your sacrifices and deceit! Your idol has no voice. Gods do not sneeze. Get Nicte! Then, and only then, I shall speak with Kulkulkan!"

"Go! Soldiers, run! I don't—ah-choo!—want to die! Hurry, before the rabbit eats up the whole sun!"

The Toltec soldiers ran helter-skelter. They were utterly terrified and quickly brought Nicte to her father. Ahcucumatz embraced his daughter.

"Please, Ahcucumatz," the high priest of Tezcatlipoca implored, "there is no time to hug. Talk to Kulkulkan. The sun is almost gone!"

Ahcucumatz looked toward his eldest son and received the signal that the eclipse was about to end. Once more Ahcucumatz prayed

Kulkulkan, god of light,
We pray you stop this deadly night.
Tezcatlipoca's had his fall.
He reigns no more in Uuc-Yab-Nal!

Miraculously, the sun reappeared in all its warmth and splendor. The crowd cheered. The high priests of Tezcatlipoca hung their heads in shame and defeat. They left the plaza as the happy crowd of people spread out and made a path for Ahcucumatz and his family. Nicte sat high on her father's shoulder as they walked home. When they arrived, he asked young Zubac, "My little son, do you still wish to be a Toltec soldier?"

Zubac, who had lived in fear throughout the past day's nightmarish events, was so relieved and happy that he marched around singing

I'll never be a Toltec soldier,
Soldier of the sacrifice.
Instead, I'll learn the mysteries
Of all the earth and of the skies!

I'll never be a Toltec soldier,
Winning power with evil lies.
Instead, I'll have the mighty wisdom,
Lasting till the ends of time!

References

Science

- Asimov, Isaac. 1920. *Asimov's New Guide to Science*. New York, Basic Books.

- ———. 1920. *Library of the Universe: The Sun*. Milwaukee, WS: Gareth Stevens.

- Davis, Don, and Anny Chantal Levasseur-Regourd. 1989. *Our Sun and the Inner Planets*. New York: Facts on File.

- Inglis, Stewart J. 1972. *Planets, Stars and Galaxies*. 3d ed. New York: John Wiley and Sons.

- Menzel, Donald H. 1975. *The Random House Illustrated Science Library*. New York: Random House.

- Pasachoff, Jay M. 1992. "The Great Eclipse: The Darkness That Enlightens." *National Geographic* 181, no. 5 (May).

- Schweighauser, Charles A. 1991. *Astronomy from A to Z*. Springfield, IL: Illinois Issues.

Anthropology

- Brecher, Kenneth, and Michael Feirtag. 1979. *Astronomy of the Ancients*. Boston: MIT Press.

- Culbert, Patrick T. 1974. *The Lost Civilization: The Story of the Classic Maya*. New York: Harper & Row.

- Demarest, Arthur A. 1993. "The Violent Saga of a Maya Kingdom," *National Geographic* 183, no. 2 (February).

- Krupp, E. C. 1983. *Echos of the Ancient Skies: The Astronomy of Lost Civilizations*. New York: Harper & Row.

- *Mysteries of the Ancient Americas: The New World Before Columbus*. 1986. New York: Reader's Digest Association.

- Roys, Ralph, L. 1967. *The Book of Chilam Balam of Chumayel*. Oklahoma City: University of Oklahoma Press.

- Weaver, Muriel Porter. 1972. *The Aztec, Maya and Their Predecessors*. New York: Seminar Press.

Folklore

- Frazer, James G. 1981. *The Golden Bough: The Roots of Religion and Folklore*. New York: Avenel Books.

- Sexton, James D., trans. and ed. 1992. *Mayan Folktales: Folklore from Lake Atitlan, Guatemala*. New York: Doubleday.

- Tedlock, Dennis, trans. 1985. *Popol Vuh*. New York: Simon & Schuster.

Music

- Gobierno Del Estado De Yucatán. *Uxmal: Luz y Sonido*. Discos LEA.

- *Modern Mayan Indian Music of Mexico*. Folkways 4377, 4379.

Zubac's Toltec Soldier Song

From "Day of the Moon Shadow"

Music and Lyrics by
JUDY GAIL

2. I'll never be a Toltec soldier,
   Soldier of the sacrifice.
   Instead, I'll learn the mysteries
   Of all the earth and of the skies!

3. I'll never be a Toltec soldier,
   Winning power with evil lies.
   Instead, I'll have the mighty wisdom,
   Lasting till the ends of time!

Song of the Clay Idol

From "Day of the Moon Shadow"

Page 1

Music and Lyrics by
JUDY GAIL

Song of the Clay Idol

From "Day of the Moon Shadow"
Page 2

March of the Toltec Priests

From "Day of the Moon Shadow"
Page 1

Music and Lyrics by
JUDY GAIL

March of the Toltec Priests

From "Day of the Moon Shadow"
Page 2

Ahcucumatz's Prayer

From "Day of the Moon Shadow"
Page 1

Music and Lyrics by
JUDY GAIL

Ahcucumatz's Prayer

From "Day of the Moon Shadow"
Page 2

kan, Tez- cat- li- po- ca, he asks on- ly for the

heart. Hear our hearts filled with light, and de-

stroy the lord of night!

autoharp   * Narration: The priests of Tezcatlipoca

ritard ------

voice (autoharp sempre simile)   autoharp

Kul- kul- kan, god of light, we pray you stop this dead- ly

night. Tez- cat- li- po- ca's had his fall. He reigns no more in Uuc-Yab-

ritard -----------

Nal!   autoharp continues

* If narration has not finished, accompanist should observe caesura.

13
THE MAGIC OF
SHAMUS O'TOOLE

THE MAGIC OF SHAMUS O'TOOLE

A Story from Ireland

How do we hear the vibrations of sound?
Without water or air, can sound travel around?
I wonder and ask, ask and wonder!

At sea level, at zero degrees Celsius, sound travels at 743 miles per hour. Its speed varies with altitude, temperature, and the medium through which it travels. Without air or water, we cannot hear sound. Air and water are called matter. Matter is any physical body in the universe, or the universe in its entirety. It occupies space and can be perceived by the senses. All matter is made up of particles called molecules. These molecules move. They vibrate.

When we talk, sing, pluck the strings of a musical instrument, bang on pots or pans, or clap our hands, cough, sneeze, cry, or laugh, molecules of air are set in motion: one pushes into another and into another and into another. This motion creates longitudinal waves, waves that travel lengthwise and carry the vibrations to our eardrums. Our brains then interpret these vibrations into what we recognize as sound. Likewise, under water, when porpoises make their many sounds and whales sing their varied songs, the molecules of water are set in motion, also in longitudinal waves. These vibrating, molecular waves allow the underwater creatures to hear sounds and communicate.

Tap a tuning fork on a table and immediately place it into a cup of water. First, you will hear the sound of the tuning fork as the molecules of air are set in motion, carrying its sound. When you dip it into the water, you will be splashed. The splash is caused by the action of a sound wave traveling through the medium of the water matter. If you throw a stone, skimming it over the water in a pond, lake, or ocean, you observe ripples spreading out and out and out, over and over until they become smaller and eventually stop. This is also what sound waves do.

An echo is created by sound waves that cannot continue to ripple out or travel because they are blocked by a barrier, such as a high mountain. The sound waves then bounce off that barrier and travel right back to whomever made the sound.

The moon has no air and no water. On the moon, you could shout, sing, play the drum, and blast loud music, but you would hear none of these sounds, for without an atmosphere of air or water, there are no molecules to vibrate and create traveling sound waves. This lack of atmosphere is called a vacuum. A device called a bell jar demonstrates how sound waves travel through air but not through a vacuum. The jar has a bell inside it, and when the jar is filled with air and the bell is rung, you can hear its ring as the air molecules are set in motion with sound waves traveling through them. A pump then draws all the air from the jar. You ring the bell, but you cannot hear its ring, for the pump has created a vacuum.

Before scientists knew about molecules, people did not know why or how sound traveled. They only knew that they could hear each other speak, hear the sounds of animals and, thus, know where to hunt or when to stay out of danger, or hear thunder, wind, rain, and all the other sounds that make up life. One of the most cherished sounds throughout the history of humankind has been that of music. The deepest human emotions have always been expressed through instruments and song.

Anciently, people often attributed magical, even supernatural, qualities to music. Listening to the beautiful notes of a flute, the beat of drums, the rhythms of rattles, or the plucking of simple string instruments, people wondered where the sound came from. Music was played and sung to gods to make them happy. Music ushered in seasons, births, weddings. It was played to send bands of hunters off with blessings of safety and a bountiful return. It could be used to communicate messages. Music inspired people to dance.

One country known for its beautiful melodies and happy dances is Ireland. It is hard to listen to an upbeat Irish jig and not start tapping your feet and rising to dance. Listening to the sweet melodies of an Irish ballad, either sung or played on the harp, can bring tears to the eyes. Irish culture is also famous for its wonderful imagination. It is difficult to find other folklore more haunted with make-believe and enchanted characters. Ireland, indeed, is a land of the weird and wonderful. Twilight is an in-between time, a time when it is not day and it is not night. Ireland is a country of cultural twilight, somewhere in between reality and the supernatural.

Irish folktales have been handed down by storytellers, or *shanachies,* for the last 2,000 years. During this time, the Irish imagination has given birth to many different fairy tale creatures. The most famous of these is certainly the leprechaun, the little shoemaker to the fairies who is the offspring of fallen angels. When people think of Ireland's "little people," those small, mischievous, yet often kind-hearted characters of make-believe, they generally think of leprechauns. Actually, the little people include all of the following: leprechauns; fairies; the *phouka*—a nightmarish horse that likes to sneak up behind unsuspecting people, toss them onto its back, and take them on a wild ride; the *banshee*—a ghostly lady of death who announces when a person is going to die by wailing and crying; *selkies*, seals who can assume human form; the headless *dullahans*; the *merrow* or mermaids; demons; ghosts; and many, many more!

Imagine yourself on the Emerald Isle, as the island of Ireland is called. Today, the people here speak English. Hundreds of years ago, they spoke in their native tongue of Gaelic. *"Erin Go Braugh"* is Gaelic for "Ireland forever!" English became the official language of Ireland when Great Britain conquered the island and ruled it.

In 1921, the Republic of Ireland gained its independence, and today Gaelic is once again taught in Irish schools.

The Irish are famous for being friendly and hospitable. They are also known to enjoy having a bit of fun with strangers and for *codding* them. Here is an example of *codding*. An Irishman comes up to you, a visitor, and says, "Ach, sure an' that's the nicest shirt I've ever seen! And such shoes, why they must have been made by the world's best shoemaker! You're such a handsome man with that thick head of hair. Why, you'd be the envy of any Irishman—now make sure ye don't go bald tomorrow—and such eyelashes—why they're longer than the lashes on me cow on the farm!" The idea is to build the person up and up. As the day goes on, the compliments become more and more ridiculous. The game ends when the stranger catches on and realizes that he or she is being teased!

Though the Irish love to laugh and play a few good-natured pranks on strangers, they are among the best hosts and hostesses you will ever find. Stop at any house, be it the poorest hut or a mansion, and the owners will most likely go out of their way to make sure you are given not only directions but also a cup of tea, a sandwich, and cakes! It would be a good idea if you could tell your hosts a story, for the Irish love a good tale. Even beggars are rewarded with food if they give their benefactors the pleasure of a fanciful story!

Imagine that one of the kind hosts warns you of the ruins of an ancient castle just down the road a little way. She advises you to stay away from it. " 'Tis haunted," she says. With that sort of encouragement, you naturally wait until twilight and head right for it! Sure enough, just as she told you, the castle stands on a rolling green hill, outlined in the darkening sky. It looks innocent enough, with gentle breezes wafting through the empty tower windows. But wait! The sound of the wind is slowing turning into music. Yes! A gentle female voice singing a beautiful love song vibrates eerily through the castle. Then, unannounced, right before your eyes, a strange little fellow dressed in green appears. He is a leprechaun! By now you are in the mood for a really good tale—and you are in luck, for sure! He is a tale-telling leprechaun!

THE MAGIC OF SHAMUS O'TOOLE

Me name is Shamus O'Toole. I've lived in this castle now for some 300 years. Hear that enchanting music? It belongs to me! This is the story from whence it came. You see, this castle used to be the busy headquarters of a large farming estate. His lordship was in charge of no fewer than 75 tenant farmers, and they all had to pay tribute to him! Now we call it "feudalism." Aye, such fancy words!

Well, 'twas the year of our Lord 1780. His lordship was away on another one of his trips to Dublin. Her ladyship, his wife, had taken over the estate in his absence. Now, she had no interest whatsoever in runnin' the estate farms, saints preserve us, no! She was more interested in controllin' a captive audience. You see, her ladyship loved to sing. Her singin' would bring tears to a grown man's eyes—and I don't mean tears of joy! Her caterwaulin' would best be compared to the bellowin' of a love-sick water buffalo!

Every Sunday, after church, she would demand the presence of all the tenant farmers from the entire estate. For three hours, she would sing, and men would bear it even though their very bones ached to the core with her horrible vibrations. Singing off-key, and as though marbles were stuck in her throat, she'd bellow out songs like this one, a standard in her dreadful repertoire:

> *Like a ship sailing on the water,*
> *My love floats all over you,*
> *But you, my dearest fishy,*
> *Do not bite upon my liiiiine.*
> *And my poor heart is brrreaking,*
> *While for only you I pine.*
> *I pi-hi-hi-hi-hi-hi-hi-hi-hi-hi-hi-ine.*
> *But you, my dearest fishy,*
> *Do not bite upon my line.*

Now, there's nothin' a leprechaun loves more than fine music—and there's nothin' he dislikes more than bad music! The only thing that kept me from removin' myself from the locale was two young people—her ladyship's daughter, Molly Maureen, and the peasant schoolmaster, Charlie. Molly Maureen had a singin' voice as fair an' lovely as her mother's was sour. And

Charlie could play the pipe and blow its sweet notes like the voice of an angel singin'. When the two of them got together, sure an' begorra, the voices of the angels couldn't of sounded sweeter! Oh, I loved the songs they'd sing and play.

Happy are the hearts that sing.
Lovely are the wee children.
Merry is the piper dear.
His pleasant music fills the air.

The hills all ring while we all sing.
The animals prance while we all dance.
As Charlie plays his pipe so fine,
The sun is smiling as it shines!

Now, Molly Maureen loved Charlie, and Charlie loved Molly Maureen. But for sure, a member of the gentry, as was Molly, couldn't marry a peasant, as was Charlie. So, their love and music were doomed. As soon as his lordship returned, Molly Maureen was to be packed up and sent off to London to find a rich and titled husband. Well, I couldn't let their sweet music end, and I couldn't stand anymore of her ladyship's singin' neither. So, I knew it was up to meself to interfere in the lives of these mortals and put things to right.

I sat and pondered and pondered and sat. Sure an', I could use me magic to turn her ladyship into the water buffalo she sounded like, but that would be too easy! 'Tis the leprechaun's way to outsmart mortals into betrayin' themselves with their own greed and conceit. Leprechauns love to watch mortals make fools of themselves. Well, I did come up with a plan. Glory be! Shamus O'Toole!—that's me, as ye know—tally be gally, what a glorious plan I concocted! I was so happy I burst into song.

Pat me back and pat me head,
I'm leprechaun green not devilish red!
I'm Shamus O'Toole, did you hear what I said?
Hoorah for the magic o' me!

Her ladyship thinks she is so smart.
She thinks she is kind at heart.
Her conceit just makes her play the fool's part!
Hoorah for the magic o' me!

From *Day of the Moon Shadow: Tales with Ancient Answers to Scientific Questions.*
©1995. Libraries Unlimited. (800) 237-6124.

Oh, Shamus O'Toole, what a wonderful plan!
A leprechaun does whatever he can.
Oh, Shamus O'Toole, I'm me own best fan!
Hoorah for the magic o' me!

And here's how me plan worked. First, I went to the castle and presented meself to her ladyship. Me gift of blarney came in handy, as I had fun *coddin'* her, knowin' her longing for compliments would render her totally unable to figure out that I just might be a'teasin' her! I lied through me teeth, flatterin' her and tellin' her what pleasure the pure tones of her magnificent voice brought to me poor humble ears. Then I said that her bell-like song needed only one thing more to transform it into perfection personified—and that was the accompaniment of a good pipe!

"Why don't ye have a contest?" says I. "First prize would be the honor of accompanyin' your ladyship on that pipe every Sunday after church. Oh, and ye can throw in the hand of yer daughter in marriage—as an added incentive."

"Oh, what a marvelous idea!" she answers me. "Shamus, you are a gen-i-us! When one is blessed with such a gift as mine, one is under obligation to enhance that gift and share it with all lesser mortals. Yes! I'll have a contest next Sunday—after church!"

Well, during the next week, the proclamation of the contest was carried throughout the land by the best horse rider and town crier as her ladyship could find. The next Sunday, no fewer than 50 excellent pipers showed up to participate. Her ladyship, naturally, thought they had all come for the honor of accompanyin' her. It never occurred to her conceited little mind that the real prize they were seeking was the hand of the fair, gentle—and rich—Molly Maureen!

Early Sunday mornin', I met with Charlie. He sat where he had been all week, under the hollyhock bush, where he was a'practicin' his pipe as if his life depended on it. His hands were shakin' with fear that someone else would be better than him—and win Molly's hand in marriage! Now, leprechauns are not known for their honest dealin's, and I am no exception. I had full intention of fixin' that contest to make sure Charlie won. Me motive was not to ensure that true love triumphed, oh, no! I intended to ensure that me favorite pastime of listenin' to the music of Molly Maureen and Charlie would always continue!

Well, maybe I am a little romantic, but mind ye, if ye ever tell anyone I said that, I'll deny it!

Now, mortals are a bit slower than leprechauns, and, at this date of 1780, they didn't understand that vibratin' air molecules cause sound, and without those air molecules, no sound can be heard. I took Charlie's pipe and worked me special magic on it. I gave it back to him and instructed him to make sure the base of the pipe was pointin' toward her ladyship when he played it. With the added confidence me magic gave him, I knew Charlie would be able to play his very best.

That afternoon, after church, all the tenant farmers gathered for the contest. They would be the ones to decide whose pipin' made her ladyship's voice sound the sweetest. The contest began. One after another, the pipers piped—and such a dreadful shame! One after another, these excellent pipers' melodious efforts were ruined by her ladyship's pitiful caterwaulin'.

Merry, merry nymphs dancing in the forest green.
Merry, merry nymphs who never can be seen.
Bring tidings of springtime love.
Paint silver clouds in the sky above.
Merry, merry nymphs who make flowers grow,
Shamrocks and heather all in a ro-ho-ho-ho-ho-ow.

Finally and last of all, it was Charlie's turn. By this time, everyone's ears were numbed with pain. The tenant farmers were beginnin' to worry who they would pick to win the contest. No one's pipin' had made her ladyship's voice sound any better than a *banshee* a'wailin'! Charlie remembered me instructions and positioned himself to the left of her ladyship and pointed the base of his pipe at her. With a glance at me and a glance at sweet Molly Maureen, he began to play. Ach! No one could play a pipe like Charlie. But more was needed to win this contest than a good—even superb—pipe player. And it was now me magic began!

From the base of the pipe, an invisible force came out and sucked in all the air molecules from around her ladyship, leavin' herself amid a vacuum. There was just a small pocket of air in the middle—so she could breathe. The additional air molecules bein' sucked into Charlie's pipe made his playin' all the more robust! Her ladyship sang and sang, and, of course, she could hear herself, but the vacuum around her prevented anyone else from hearin' her. When they heard Charlie's pipe, the tired farmers were confused. They watched her ladyship move her mouth, breathe in and out, make her grand gestures but—no sound came out! She looked a bit like the "fishy in the water" of her song.

Well, the tenant farmers loved Charlie's music so that they soon began to laugh and clap and dance. When Charlie blew his last note, the vacuum disappeared! It was obvious from the reaction of the farmers whose pipin' had made her ladyship's voice sound the sweetest. Not realizin' that the farmers' consensus was that the sweetest sound from her vocal chords was no sound at all, and not realizin' that a trick had been played on her, a very pleased her ladyship gave Molly Maureen's hand in marriage to Charlie, with the condition that he accompany her singin' every Sunday after church! The tenant farmers cheered. It would be no trouble listenin' to Charlie's playin' while watchin' her ladyship's silent lips move!

When his lordship returned from England, he was enraged to hear that his daughter was to marry a common schoolmaster. Ho! But when he heard—or rather couldn't hear—her ladyship's caterwaulin' every Sunday after church, he was overjoyed! And Charlie's magnificent pipin' pleased his educated and cultured ears. So, all was well, thanks to me magic. And what a fine weddin' was that of Molly and Charlie. What music the two played.

What happiness it brought to me leprechaun ears and heart. "Ah, Shamus," I couldn't stop pattin' meself on me back. "You did it again," I said to meself. "You did it so cleverly!"

Well, Charlie and Molly Maureen made sweet music together for the rest of their lives. And although they've both long since gone to join the angels, I've kept some of their music to give me comfort. Now, if you are brave enough to visit the castle at twilight, and you stand real quiet, you can hear their happy songs of love driftin' through the air, over the stones of the castle, and out over the meadows where they danced.

Wherever we be, we will always be together,
For our hearts beat as one in any wind or weather.
And our love fills the air with music bright and clear,
And so it shall be for year after year.

With a tally rally hey and a ho!
With a rangle, jangle jiggle a jo!
With a tally rally hey and a ho
For sweet Molly Maureen and her dear Charlie O!

References

Science

- Brandt, Keith. 1985. *Sound*. Mahwah, NJ: Troll.

- Branley, Franklyn Mansfield, and Paul Galdone. 1967. *High Sounds, Low Sounds*. New York: Thomas Y. Crowell.

- Brinton, Henry. 1966. *Sound: What It Is and How We Hear It* (Finding Out About Science series). New York: Golden Press.

- Heur, Kenneth. 1981. *Thunder, Singing Sands and Other Wonders: Sounds in the Atmosphere*. New York: Dodd, Mead.

- Miller, Dayton Clarence, *Sound Waves: Their Shape and Speed*. New York: Macmillan, 1937.

Anthropology

- de Breffny, Brian. 1977. *Castles of Ireland*. London: Thames and Hudson.

- *Encyclopedia of Ireland*. 1968. New York: McGraw-Hill.

- Fairclough, Chris. 1986. *We Live in Ireland*. New York: Bockwright Press.

- Grant, Neil. 1989. *Ireland*. Englewood Cliffs, NJ: Silver Burdett Press.

- Haining, Peter. 1980. *The Leprechaun's Kingdom*. New York: Harmony Books.

- MacCana, Proinsias. 1985. *Celtic Mythology*. New York: Bedrick Books.

- Macdonagh, Michael. 1905. *Irish Life and Character*. Hodder and Stoughton.

Folklore

- Flood, William Henry Grattan. [1913.] 1970. *A History of Irish Music*. Reprint, New York: Praeger.

- Glassie, Henry, ed. 1985. *Irish Folk Tales*. New York: Pantheon.

- Mac Con Iomaire, Liam. 1988. *Ireland of the Proverb*. Grand Rapids, MI: Masters Press.

- MacManus, Seumas, reteller. 1968. *Donegal Fairy Stories*. New York: Dover.

- O'Hanlon, John. 1977. *Irish Folklore: Traditions and Superstitions of the Country with Humorous Tales*. Norwood, PA: Norwood Editions.

Music

- The Bothy Band. *Afterhours*. Green Linnet Records. CSIF 3016.

- Cole, William, ed. 1961. *Folksongs of England, Ireland, Scotland & Wales*. New York: Doubleday.

- The Irish Rovers. *The Life of a Rover*. Decca Records.

Her Ladyship's Song

From "The Magic of Shamus O'Toole"

Music and Lyrics by
JUDY GAIL

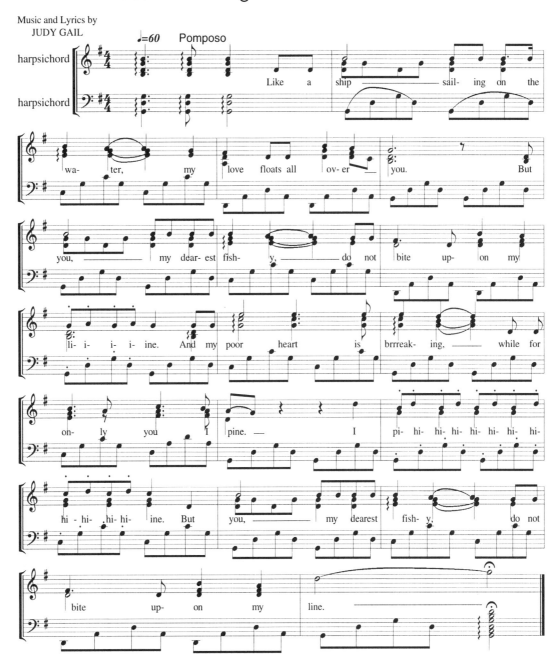

Molly's Song

From "The Magic of Shamus O'Toole"

Music and Lyrics by
JUDY GAIL

2. The hills all ring while we all sing.
   The animals prance while we all dance.
   As Charlie plays his pipe so fine,
   The sun is smiling as it shines!

The Leprechaun's Song

From "The Magic of Shamus O'Toole"

Music and Lyrics by
JUDY GAIL

The Contest Song: Merry, Merry Nymphs

From "The Magic of Shamus O'Toole"

Music and Lyrics by
JUDY GAIL

Segue into "FLUTE MUSIC"

Flute Music

From "The Magic of Shamus O'Toole"

Music and Lyrics by
JUDY GAIL

"Flute Music" should be repeated as many times as necessary to accomodate narration.

From *Day of the Moon Shadow: Tales with Ancient Answers to Scientific Questions.* ©1995. Libraries Unlimited. (800) 237-6124. Copyright ©1987, ©1995, Poppykettle Enterprises, Inc., Miami, Florida. (305) 387-3683. International copyrights secured. All rights reserved.

Ode to Molly Maureen and Charlie

From "The Magic of Shamus O'Toole"

Music and Lyrics by
JUDY GAIL

Shamus's Ode to Molly Maureen and Charlie

From "The Magic of Shamus O'Toole"

Music and Lyrics by
JUDY GAIL

With a tal- ly ral- ly hey and a ho! With a rang- le, jang- le jig- gle a jo! With a tal- ly ral- ly hey and a ho for sweet Mol- ly Maur- een and her dear Char- lie O!

14
HELGA THE HOWLER

A Viking Adventure

How did people sail on the oceans
With no compass, computer, or ship-to-shore telephones?
I wonder and ask, ask and wonder!

Many animals have a natural sense of direction. Salmon return from the ocean to the exact spot in the river where they were hatched. Whales and seals swim thousands of miles to warmer waters each fall as the seasons change, then return home in the spring. The annual migration of lobsters is an amazing spectacle, as these creatures crawl over the ocean floor, following their leader, the largest lobster, with absolute precision to their mating and seasonal grounds: warmer waters in winter, cooler waters in summer. Migratory birds fly thousands of miles without getting lost, and many return to the same trees or nesting spots during each migration. Stories have been told of missing dogs and cats that instinctively found their way home.

We humans, who can speak, write, read, make tools, build pyramids and skyscrapers, and invent computers, have not been blessed with this homing instinct. We must rely instead on our learned abilities to find our way around. This knowledge is the science of navigation. Navigation comes from a Latin root word that means both ship and move. Through the centuries, people have invented many tools to help them find their way from one place to another. The compass, certainly the most widely used navigational tool, originated in ancient China.

Around 100 B.C., the Chinese observed that the lodestone, a natural magnet, always pointed north when suspended in air. Until this time, people had to rely on the North Star for direction, and this was no help during the day or in cloudy weather. The lodestone was not very accurate. Neither were the first compasses. It took centuries of experimentation to develop an accurate and reliable compass. Around A.D. 200, sailors began to make compasses by inserting a magnetic needle through a piece of straw and floating it in a bowl of water. Later, this was improved by attaching the needle to a card with the directions north, south, east, and west.

We know today that, to be accurate, compasses must be protected from magnetic fields that surround us. On today's large metal ships, a magnetic compass is of little use, for the metal distorts accuracy. Most large ships rely on an electrically driven heavy wheel that spins on an axle. This is a gyrocompass. Whatever direction the ship is sailing, the axle adjusts itself so that it always points due north.

A sailing tool called an astrolabe consists of a metal disk marked with a scale around it, containing a map of the stars. A bar with a pointer and sighting holes is attached to the disk's center. The bar can be rotated until the sighting holes line up with the night's stars. A reading is then taken from the scale that tells the height of the stars above the horizon.

Another navigational instrument that indicates the height of stars above the horizon is the quadrant. Shaped like a quarter circle, it has a scale along its rounded edge. This scale indicates the angle of particular stars, and this angle helps to determine both distance and direction from certain points.

The sextant measures latitude and longitude and tells location north, south, east, or west by degrees.

Today navigation is also aided by radio waves. A looped antenna can detect the direction from which a radio wave is traveling and let a ship know the exact whereabouts of another ship. Satellites help by broadcasting details of their orbits by a signal code and Doppler information, which indicates location through sound frequencies. This information is fed into computers aboard ships and lets them know precisely where they are at sea. Today, the oceans are mapped, charted, and traveled daily with the many excellent, accurate navigational instruments resulting from research and discoveries.

There was a time, long ago, when there were no compasses, sextants, radio antennas, satellites, or computers. Yet people still sailed the seas. How?

One thousand years ago, the Vikings, from what are now Denmark, Sweden, and Norway, sailed their ships to Iceland, Greenland, Great Britain, France, Russia, and even North America—500 years before Columbus sailed to the Americas! During the Viking era, it was not yet known that the world was round. People believed it to be flat, and sailors feared falling off the edge. Brave, hardy, no-nonsense Vikings did not let this fear stop them from sailing! Nor were they hindered by their belief in ferocious giants who represented everything evil in nature. According to Viking lore, the way to destroy a giant was not to let him know of your fear. Instead, bravely defy him and laugh in his face, for then he will melt into a blob of glop!

To the Vikings, nothing was more important than their ships. These magnificently constructed sailing vessels were up to 65 feet long and 6 to 9 feet deep. They had sails but were more often powered by long, sturdy oars rowed by thralls, slaves captured from the many lands where the Vikings sailed. Each ship had a special figurehead carved in the likeness of an animal. A Viking would not set sail until a ceremony was held in which a protective spirit was summoned into the figurehead, such as the spirit of the wolf or bear. These spirits would guard the sailors on their journeys. Vikings also would never dock a ship without first removing the figurehead if it had an open mouth or fangs, for this, they believed, would offend the spirits of the land.

A Viking village included a sacrificial grove where, once every nine years a nine-day sacrifice was held. At this time animals and people were killed and hung in trees. The Vikings believed that as the birds pecked at the dead bodies, they would pluck out each soul and carry it to the gods, making them happy. Thus, the gods would see to it that the Vikings were safe at sea.

These brave sailors used a secret discovered in nature itself—the sun stone! This calcite mineral normally appears as a gray-toned crystal. However, according to Viking legend, it glows blue when pointed at the sun. The sun stone enabled Vikings to locate the sun and, subsequently, identify east and west on days when the sky was completely overcast.

Viking maps resembled maps for treasure hunts. Let's say they wanted to reach Norkey Island. The map would say the following:

"Follow the Shetlands so far to the north that its hills will be exactly half visible. Once you have found this landmark, look for a tree that lightning has split in half. Now, use the sun stone and turn west. Follow the setting sun westward until birds and dolphins greet you. They will lead you to Norkey Island."

Imagine yourself in Norway in a Viking village by the cold waters of the North Atlantic. You are dressed in bearskin clothing and, with the other villagers, are gathering inside the Thing, which is what Vikings called their central meeting house. Here, the villagers make important decisions about planting, hunting, and, most important, ship building and sailing ventures. In this meeting house, celebrations and communal feasts are held, and storytellers called *skalds* tell and sing of their adventures and those of others. *Skalds* are famous for their alliteration, or stories filled with words beginning with the same sound. Tonight, let's suspend the restraints of time and pretend that the centuries have come together. Helga the Howler is entertaining us with the remarkable tale of how she earned her name!

Helga the Howler

I won my name of Helga the Howler on the grim, gray, great North Atlantic by the time I was 16 years of age. Until that age, we Viking maidens were most often warrior maidens. Then, we had to choose between marriage or a life at sea. Sometimes, we could indulge in both. It was an honor to be domestic, for we women ruled the village and ran our households. We wore big key chains around our waists as symbols of the great powers we held. Why, we could swing an ax as well as any man. We, too, fought to conquer, to defend ourselves, and to survive.

I hear they call our times the Dark Ages, implying we were ignorant. I disagree! "Helga the Howler," I hear you say. "That is the name of a barbarian." And you've heard of others among us. There was Ragnar Hairy Breeches, who was smart enough to invent fireproof pants, and Harold Bluetooth, known for his intelligence—as well as his bad blue teeth. Remember Olaf the Stout, who, in battle, pulled London Bridge down? Ho, ho, you still sing the song "London Bridge is falling down." Oh, yes, there were the Eriksons—Lief and his son, Erik the Red, who reached America long before Columbus. But you want to know why I am called Helga the Howler. To learn the answer, come with me beyond the horizon as we go Viking!

Hoist the sail and away we go.
Where we go we do not know.
Hoist the sail and ev'ryone sing,
And come with me as we go Viking!

Hoist the sail and ev'ryone row.
Where we row we do not know.
Ev'ryone row and ev'ryone sing,
And come with me as we go Viking!
And come with me as we go Viking!

Our ship has been built under the skilled hand of Brivaard the Barnacle. Brivaard has spent so many years at sea—sailing, swimming, and slipping on barnacled rocks—that his sea-weathered skin has grown barnacles. In his hair they look like jagged jewels that have lost their sparkle to the sea salt of the salty sea. Brivaard has built a ship with 18 oars on each side and a depth of nearly nine feet. The only tasks that remain are for the figurehead to be placed on the prow and for us to summon its spirit within to protect us. Our figurehead is that of a wolf, an animal with wisdom, strength, dignity, and loyalty—certainly an animal capable of protecting us.

We are about to begin this sacred ceremony. It is a good omen that this has been the year of the nine-year sacrifice. Birds that have come from the sacrificial grove are flying overhead, carrying the soul offerings to the gods. We have just placed our wolf on the prow when, impatient and forever hungry, Trigivv Olafson foolishly shoots his spear at a bird! The bird falls to the ground dead, near our magnificent wolf. We did not know it at the time, but, as the bird fell, the sacrificed soul it had been carrying to the gods left the bird and entered our figurehead, leaving no room for our wolf spirit. That would be sure to bring trouble!

All is packed: our tents, food, mead wine, skins, furs. The air is filled with excitement and fear. The sail carries us out to sea, for the wind is in our favor. Ah! The wonderful smell of salt air fills every happy, seafaring nose.

Then, suddenly, lightning flashes. This means the trolls are fighting with the giants! We hear the loud hammering of Thor, the thunder god. Thor is known as a protector. He should be happy. Sacrifices have been made. But no! Huge waves swirl around us. One harrowing horror follows another. Our wolf figurehead begins to cry. Never before have we heard a figurehead make noises. The thunderous slapping and splashing of waves threatens to rip Brivaard's beautiful ship apart, and many oars crack while the rudder becomes useless under the weight of the waters. We hear the eerie echo of the Man of Corpses giving his count of pirates and sailors washed onto his island to be buried in his caves.

"We are nearing the land where the giants fight with the trolls!" Brivaard yells over the whooshing and whipping of the angry sea. "Remember, hardy Vikings, a Viking must be defiant in the face of danger and death!"

Brothers and comrades, yes, all of the crew,
Remember we're Vikings and do what we do.
Laugh and defy the giants we fear,
And you'll see their powers will all disappear!

Brothers and comrades, don't dare shed one tear.
A hardy, strong Viking will never show fear.
Giants are real, but so is our might.
So call on your courage, yes, Vikings—go FIGHT!

"Wah—wah—huh—wah," the cry comes from our figurehead. We are all thrown to the bottom of the boat and are certain we have reached the horizon and are falling off the edge of the world. What lies over the edge of the world? We are flung, flying, out of the ship onto land. Our ship has been beached before we could remove the figurehead. What else could go wrong? This means certain doom. The peaceful spirits of the forests and gardens will be angered by the wolf's fangs and rise up disturbed. Unbelievable! As quickly as the storm arose, it now ends, and the sun shines. Oh, oh, no! Giants surround us, smiling, smirking, showing us their sword-like teeth. Their hands hold huge clubs and axes, and their booming voices hurt our ears as they chant

From *Day of the Moon Shadow: Tales with Ancient Answers to Scientific Questions.*
©1995. Libraries Unlimited. (800) 237-6124.

We are the giants, we fight with the trolls,
But Vikings are far more to our likings!
We bring the storms and all the fright'ning things
From which ev'ry terrifying nightmare springs!
With a YO! and a HO! We giants always know
How to toss you to and fro,
How your course to overthrow
As a Viking you must go!
With a YO! HO! HO! HO! YO! HO! HO! HO! HO!
As a Viking you must go!

They are coming after us. There is nothing we can do except not show our fear. I crawl near the ship and cannot believe my eyes or ears. Our figurehead is groaning like a ghost! Suddenly, I remember! Suddenly, it all becomes clear to me. The bird! Yes! The bird that was shot down by Viking Olafson. Can it really be? Yes! The bird was carrying a sacrificed soul from

the sacrificial grove. This soul is what has entered our wolf, not the spirit of the wolf! The gods are angry at us, very angry. They think we are thieves. We stole a gift meant for them!

A giant is moving toward our ship. To him it will be a toy to pick up and throw. I hear Brivaard defying another giant with sharp words. But there are too many giants for us to defy them all, to laugh in each one's face. My hand is powerful. My battle ax is in my belt. I know there is only one thing to be done. I must crack open the hard oak wood of the figurehead and release the imprisoned spirit Oh, no! A giant is lifting his foot up over me. He is about to step on me and crush me like an ant!

Quickly, I squat, and then, with every bit of Viking defiance of danger and death, I push myself off the ground and jump nine feet into the air, diving into the boat. I remove my battle ax from my belt. In one strong stroke, I crack open the figurehead. The imprisoned soul whispers to me, "You have freed me—I will carry the message of your wisdom and good deed to the gods."

I am grateful for the words the spirit has spoken, but there is no time to waste between now and the spirit's reaching Asir, the land where the gods dwell. Quickly, I crawl into the crevice under our figurehead and imagine hard that I am a wolf. It is then that I begin to howl.

> *Ah-ooo Ah-ooo Ah-ooo!*
> *I am a wolf, I am smaller than you.*
> *Giants are clumsy oafs,*
> *I move faster than you do.*
> *Ah-ooo Ah-ooo Ah-ooo!*
>
> *I will nibble on your toes*
> *And right up to your nose.*
> *I'll devour you as sure*
> *As the ocean always flows.*
> *Ahooo Ahooo Ahooo!*

The giants run helter-skelter with gigantic terror at the hoot of the howls. The crew does as the wolf commands. They believe that the gods are now helping and have sent us here for the purpose of destroying the giants and winning a battle for the gods. Their Viking bravery at defying their fears sends the giants' power into the air. In an instant, 100 fierce giants begin to shrink, their bones bending and breaking. They lose all form and look like an island of jellyfish. The hot sun melts them all!

I climb out of the ship and join my fellow Vikings on the shore. Brivaard sees me and says, "Helga, where have you been? I thought for sure the giants had captured you—but that would not be like you, my brave comrade. Where were you?"

It is then that I tell them the story of the imprisoned soul and how I set it free—and how I howled and yowled and howled in defiance of the giants. It is then that they name me—Helga the Howler!

And it is then that Brivaard and I get married, to spend our lives sailing on the wonderful oceans together! We repair our ship and set sail for other shores with the sun, stars, and moon, the wind, waves, and whales as our guides. Yes, giants and trolls frighten us. You modern people have gremlins of your own. For us, the seas are as unknown as outer space is for you! When you think of us Vikings, do not think of us as ignorant. Instead, think of your joys—and fears—when you venture beyond the horizon to another planet. What kinds of creatures might you encounter there? Giants, perhaps? Whatever, follow the driving wonder to explore. Never be afraid to go Viking!

> *Hoist the sail and away we go.*
> *Where we go we do not know.*
> *Hoist the sail and everyone sing,*
> *Go where you must, yes, go Viking!*

References

Science

- Branley, Franklyn Mansfield. 1966. *North, South, East and West*. New York: Crowell.

- Eyster, William. 1970. *Thataway: The Story of the Magnetic Compass*. New York: A. S. Barnes.

- Harre, Rom. 1981. *Great Scientific Experiments*. Oxford: Phaidon Press.

- Hellman, Hal. 1966. *Navigation: Land, Sea, and Sky*. Englewood Cliffs, NJ: Prentice-Hall.

- Hogan, Paula. 1982. *The Compass*. New York: Walker.

- *Illustrated Encyclopedia of Science*. 1984. New York: Exeter Books.

- *Magnets and Magnetism*. 1963. (The How and Why Wonder series). New York: Grosset & Dunlap.

- Morris, William, ed. 1981. *The American Heritage Dictionary*. Boston: Houghton Mifflin.

Anthropology

- Brondstad, Johannes. 1960. *The Vikings*. Baltimore, Md.: Penguin Books.

- La Fay, Howard. 1972. *The Vikings*. Washington, DC: National Geographic Society.

- Magnusson, Magnus. 1976. *Hammer of the North*. New York: Putnam.

- Olrik, Axel. 1930. *Viking Civilization*. New York: The American-Scandinavian Foundation; W. W. Norton.

Folklore

- Craigie, Sir William Alexander. 1970. *Scandinavian Folklore: Traditional Beliefs of the Northern Peoples*. Singing Tree Press.

- Guerber, H. A. *The Norsemen*. London: Studio Editions, 1993.

- Leach, Maria, and Jerome Fried, eds. 1950. *Standard Dictionary of Folklore, Mythology & Legend*. New York: Funk and Wagnalls.

- Rugoff, Milton, ed. 1949. *A Harvest of World Folktales*. New York: Viking.

- Wright, Rachel. 1992. *Vikings: Facts, Things to Make, Activities*. New York: Franklin Watts.

Music

- *Music from the Orkney Islands*. Folkways FW 8470.

- Sibelius, *Finlandia* and *The Swan of Tuonela*. EMI 4AE -34491.

- *Songs and Pipes of the Hebrides*. Folkways FE 4430.

Go Viking

From "Helga the Howler"

Music and Lyrics by
JUDY GAIL

Guitar with low E-string tuned down
to D makes a good accompaniment.

Verse 3 is sung at the end of the story.

Hoist the sail and away we go.
Where we go we do not know.
Hoist the sail and everyone sing,
Go where you must, yes, go Viking!

From *Day of the Moon Shadow: Tales with Ancient Answers to Scientific Questions.* ©1995. Libraries Unlimited. (800) 237-6124. Copyright ©1987, ©1995, Poppykettle Enterprises, Inc., Miami, Florida. (305) 387-3683. International copyrights secured. All rights reserved.

Brivaard's Song of Defiance

From "Helga the Howler"

Music and Lyrics by
JUDY GAIL

Song of the Giants

From "Helga the Howler"

Helga's Howl

From "Helga the Howler"

Music and Lyrics by
JUDY GAIL

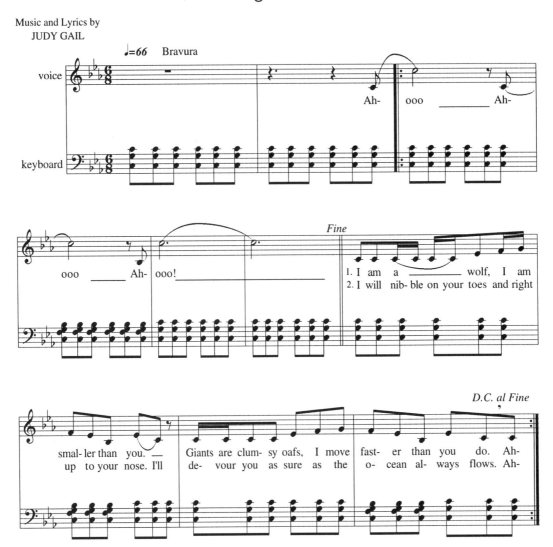

APPENDIX A: SUGGESTED STORYTELLING GUIDES

- Hamilton, Martha, and Mitch Weiss. 1990. *Children Tell Stories*. Katonah, NY: Richard C. Owen.

- Haven, Kendall. 1994. *Marvels of Science: 50 Fascinating 5-Minute Reads*. Englewood, CO: Libraries Unlimited.

- Moore, Robin. 1991. *Awakening the Hidden Storyteller: How to Build a Storytelling Tradition in Your Family*. Boston: Shambala.

- *National Storytelling Directory*. 1976-present. Jonesborough, TN: The National Storytelling Association. This thorough directory lists storytellers; workshops; publications; local storytelling associations and events across the nation and abroad; and suggested reading and award-winning storytelling books, tapes, and videos.

- Nelson, Pat. 1993. *Magic Minutes: Quick Read-Alouds for Every Day*. Englewood, CO: Libraries Unlimited.

- Pellowski, Anne. 1990. *Hidden Stories in Plants: Unusual and Easy-to-Tell Stories from Around the World Together with Creative Things to Do While Telling Them*. New York: Macmillan.

- *Storytelling Magazine*. 1975-present. Jonesborough, TN: The National Storytelling Association. This is a bi-monthly publication filled with professional articles about storytelling and related activities.

Judy Gail, called the *pisc* (mouth) of her family, was born a storyteller. Both of her parents were musicians, and her father was long-time director of children's records at Columbia, so it was natural that Judy also became a musician and balladeer. She earned her B.A. in theatre arts and education from Sarah Lawrence College and pursued a career performing original entertaining educational programs.

As Musical Director for the Shadow Box Theatre in Manhattan for seven years, Judy created voice-overs for a host of characters and served as a one-woman band and vocalist. During her four years as Director of Live Science at the Miami Museum of Science, she researched, wrote, and performed 25 live science demonstrations that included her original stories and songs. Since then, Judy has written and produced a television documentary targeting teenagers on the topic of AIDS; created and produced the television special "Hurricane at the Zoo," for which she wrote the theme song and co-authored the healing tale with Linda A. Houlding; appeared as guest storyteller on the series Once Upon a Time, Time; and continues to freelance as a writer, a producer, and always, a storyteller/balladeer. Judy is also the founder of Poppykettle Enterprises. Those wishing to obtain audiocassettes of the 10 tales not included on the Libraries Unlimited cassette may purchase additional tapes directly from Poppykettle Enterprises, Inc., 13411 SW 112th Ln., Miami, FL 33186, (305) 387-3683.

Judy has four children and two grandchildren and lives in Miami with her husband, Dr. Mark J. Hagmann, a scientist and professor.

Linda A. Houlding grew up on the south side of Chicago, in a neighborhood where interracial violence was prevalent. She learned, firsthand, how prejudicial hatred can permanently scar young minds and hearts. Today, as an anthropologist, Linda enjoys using the exciting medium of storytelling to help people of different cultures better understand and appreciate each other.

Linda earned a B.S. in prehistoric archaeology and an M.S. in cultural anthropology from Brigham Young University. Her areas of specialization include Native North American sociopolitical organizations and interpreting information for the public in comprehensible, interest-arousing scripts and displays. She was an exhibit designer for three years at the BYU Museum of Peoples and Cultures and Curator of Natural History for nine years at the Miami Museum of Science, where she designed and built the Collections Gallery and created associated educational programs.

Linda taught anthropology at Chapman University, Edwards Air Force Base in California. Currently, she lives in Misowa, Japan, with her husband Charles, a USAF medical officer, and their two sons.

Other storytelling and multicultural books and resources from Libraries Unlimited:

- **Clever Folk: Tales of Wisdom, Wit, and Wonder.** By Ruthilde M. Kronberg. 1993. 1-56308-139-3.

- **The Corn Woman: Audio Stories and Legends of the Hispanic Southwest, English and Spanish Versions.** World Folklore Series. 1995. English, 1-56308-394-9; Spanish, 1-56308-395-7; Both, 1-56308-396-5.

- **The Corn Woman: Stories and Legends of the Hispanic Southwest.** By Angel Vigil. World Folklore Series. 1994. 1-56308-194-6.

- **Folk Stories of the Hmong: Peoples of Laos, Thailand, and Vietnam.** By Norma J. Livo and Dia Cha. World Folklore Series. 1991. 0-87287-854-6.

- **Hyena and the Moon: Stories to Listen to from Kenya.** World Folklore Series. 1995. 1-56308-397-3.

- **Hyena and the Moon: Stories to Tell from Kenya.** By Heather McNeil. World Folklore Series. 1994. 1-56308-169-5.

- **Images of a People: Tlingit Myths and Legends.** By Mary Helen Pelton and Jacqueline DiGennaro. World Folklore Series. 1992. 0-87287-918-6.

- **Marvels of Science: 50 Fascinating 5-Minute Reads.** By Kendall Haven. 1994. 1-56308-159-8.

- **One Voice: Music and Stories in the Classroom.** By Barbara M. Britsch and Amy Dennison-Tansey. 1995. 1-56308-049-4.

- **Thai Tales: Folktales of Thailand.** Retold by Supaporn Vathanaprida. Edited by Margaret Read MacDonald. World Folklore Series. 1994. 1-56308-096-6.

- **Who's Afraid . . . ? Facing Children's Fears with Folktales.** By Norma J. Livo. 1994. 0-87287-950-X.

- **Wise Women: Folk and Fairy Tales from Around the World.** By Suzanne I. Barchers. 1990. 0-87287-816-3.

- **Wonder Beasts: Tales and Lore of the Phoenix, the Griffin, the Unicorn, and the Dragon.** By Joe Nigg. 1995. 1-56308-242-X.

Call 1-800-237-6124 for a free catalog or a storytelling brochure.